uu&me!

D1449729

Eastrose Fellowship
Unitarian Universalist
1133 NE 181st Ave
Portland, OR 97230
503.665.2628

R. E.

uu &me!

Collected Stories

Betsy Hill Williams, Editor

SKINNER HOUSE BOOKS
BOSTON

Copyright © 2003 by the Unitarian Universalist Association of
Congregations. Published by Skinner House Books. Skinner House Books
is an imprint of the Unitarian Universalist Association of Congregations, a
liberal religious organization with more than 1,000 congregations in the
U.S. and Canada. 25 Beacon St., Boston, MA 02108-2800.

Cover design and text design by Kathryn Sky-Peck.
Printed in Canada.
ISBN 1-55896-455-X
978-1-55896-455-6
09 08 07
10 9 8 7 6 5 4 3 2

Library of Congress Cataloging-in-Publication Data

UU and me collected stories / Betsy Williams, editor.
      p. cm.
    Summary: A collection of short stories, historical articles, and
    biographical sketches, selected from the children's magazine "uu&me!,"
    that illustrate Unitarian Universalist principles and values.
      ISBN 1-55896-455-X (alk. paper)
      1. Unitarian Universalist Association—Literary collections.
    [1. Unitarian Universalist Association—Literary collections.]
    I. Williams, Betsy.
    PZ5.U85 2003
    242--dc21   2003042707

"The Preacher, the Farmer, and the Little Church That Waited" is adapted
from a story in the *UU Kids Book* by Charlene Brotman et al.
Brotman-Marshfield, 1989.
"The Floating Bridge of Heaven" is adapted from a story in *Beginnings:
Earth, Sky, Life, Death* by Sophia Lyon Fahs and Dorothy T. Spoerl.
Starr King Press, 1958.

Contents

Tales of Yesterday and Today

Raychel and Tony

Judith C. Campbell

Introduction

For over fifty years, the Church of the Larger Fellowship (CLF) has brought Unitarian Universalism into the homes of isolated Unitarian Universalist families around the world. Starting in the 1950s, religious education for CLF families came in the form of regular mailings from the Boston office: Church School by Mail, as it was called, included adaptations of the Beacon curriculum series for home use and two periodicals, *Junior News* for children and *Uniteen* for youth. Over the years the form and content of CLF's mailings to families changed with the times: only *Junior News* survived into the 1990s, when it was finally given a face-lift, a new name, and a denomination-wide audience. The stories in this collection are taken from the first five years of the new publication, *uu&me!*, a Unitarian Universalist Magazine for Kids.

With *uu&me!*, the audience broadened to include UU kids everywhere but the mission of the publication remained the same: to bring the values and principles of Unitarian Universalism into the everyday lives of children. The stories in *uu&me!* are fictional and factual, historical and modern, mythical and true-life. They are chosen for their power to spark imaginations and stimulate reflection on what really matters and how our faith informs our daily lives.

This collection is divided into three sections. In the first section, *Our Faith Heritage,* biographical sketches of significant historical figures are presented in the context of enduring Unitarian Universalist values and principles. The reader will learn about Joseph Priestley's search for truth, Clara Barton's courage, and King John Sigismund's unique religious tolerance. They will learn about how John Murray brought Universalism to America—in three different treatments. One is a mini-biography of Murray himself, another is an "interview" with the builder of the first church where Murray preached, and the third is a short story about a fictional family setting off to hear the first Universalist sermon preached in America. Other stories in this section explore the roots of current Unitarian Universalist practices, such as chalice lighting and international partnering with the Partner Church Council. The image of kids who share our faith heritage is expanded when we meet Bettje, a young Unitarian from the village of Kadacs, in "Here They Come! A Visit to Transylvania."

The second section is a collection of fictional stories that reflect Unitarian Universalist values in both mythical and real-life settings. Love resolves sibling rivalry in the classic Japanese creation story "The Floating Bridge of Heaven," and again in the modern Christmas tale "Don't Smash Santa." Finding goodness and strength in adversity are common themes: The water bearer grows a beautiful garden when his jug develops a crack, a good day turns bad and a young boy learns not to jump to conclusions and blame himself, and a devoted daughter learns to see beauty and love in her hands—and in herself—where once she saw only shame.

Almost every issue of *uu&me!* has a story about Raychel and her cousin Tony, two fictional Unitarian Universalist kids who discover how being UU makes a difference in their lives. The final section is a collection from this continuing series. Themes and conflicts common to children today provide the backdrop for exploring choices and understanding how the choices we make connect with our values and beliefs. In "One of Us," Raychel wants so desperately to be accepted into a girls' club that she is caught stealing a scarf. Tony learns a valuable lesson about self-respect and trying your best from a cabin-mate in "Two for One Summer." In "An Almost Awful Holiday," Raychel and her family help her friend Sooze find a way to enjoy the holidays after her parents' divorce. "Free to Believe," "Courage to Create," and "All You Had to Do Was Ask" invite children to think about how they are called to the same values of courage, honesty, and tolerance that were introduced by the historical figures in the first section.

Like Unitarian Universalism itself, these stories are diverse in content and style but share a common grounding in the search for truth, beauty, and love. Read them aloud and discover what thoughts and feelings they uncover for you and your family. Use them as a tool for learning more about our faith heritage. Or simply leave them on the bedside table of a young reader in your life. The child you give this collection to is sure to discover, as Raychel and Tony do, what it means to be a Unitarian Universalist kid.

Our
Faith
Heritage

The Healing Cup

The Story of the Flaming Chalice

Many Unitarian Universalist churches and fellowships start their worship service on Sunday morning by lighting a flame inside a chalice. This flaming chalice is a symbol for Unitarian Universalists just as the cross and the Star of David are symbols for other religious groups. The story of how the flaming chalice became our symbol is an interesting one and it begins during the Second World War.

During that war, a lot of people living in Eastern Europe—Unitarians, Jews, and others—were in danger of being put in prison or killed by Nazi soldiers. A group of Unitarians came together in Boston, Massachusetts, to form the Unitarian Service Committee and their plan was to help the people in danger from the Nazis. The director of the Service Committee was the Unitarian minister Charles Joy. Rev. Joy had an office in Portugal so he would be near the people he wanted to help. He was in charge of a whole secret group of agents and messengers who worked hard trying to find safe routes for people to escape.

Rev. Joy and his assistants often needed to ask governments and other organizations for their help to save people who were in danger. They would send messages to anyone in government who might give them money, transportation, or a safe route. Because they were a new organization though, not very many people had heard of them. This made it much harder for Rev. Joy and the people in the Unitarian Service Committee to get the help they needed.

In those days during the war, when danger was everywhere, lots of people were running away from their own countries. Often, people who were escaping and people who wanted to help didn't speak the same language. Rev. Joy decided it would be much better if the Service Committee had an official symbol, or picture, to help identify its members. With a picture or symbol, it wouldn't matter if people couldn't read the language.

It looked like Rev. Joy would need to find an artist. He went to a very talented man named Hans Deutsch for help. Deutsch had escaped from the Nazis in Paris, France, where he was in danger because he drew cartoons showing people how evil the Nazis were. Rev. Joy asked Deutsch to create a symbol to print on Service Committee papers to make them look important. He wanted the symbol to impress governments and police who had the power to help move people to safety.

For his drawing, Deutsch borrowed an old symbol of strength and freedom from Czechoslovakia—a chalice with a flame. Rev. Joy wrote to his friends in Boston that the new symbol seemed to show the real spirit of the Unitarian religion. It showed a chalice, or cup, that was used for giving a healing drink to others. And it showed a flame on top of the chalice because a flame was often used to represent a spirit of helpfulness and sacrifice. And so the flaming chalice became the official symbol of the Unitarian Service Committee.

Many years later, the flaming chalice became the symbol of Unitarian Universalist groups all over the world. By the early 1970s, enough Unitarian Universalists had heard the story of the flaming chalice symbol that they began to light a flaming chalice as part of the worship service in their churches. Over the years, this practice has spread over most of the United States and Canada.

What does it mean to have a symbol like this? Well, one thing it means is that wherever you see a flaming chalice, you know that there are Unitarians and Universalists nearby. Having a symbol also can remind you of what's most important to you—and sometimes a reminder can make a very big difference.

One very old woman told how the flaming chalice of her homeland, Czechoslovakia, helped her while she was in a Nazi prison camp. Printed under the picture of the Czech flaming chalice was the motto "pravda vitezi," which means, in English, "truth overcomes," or "truth prevails." Every single morning in that terrible camp, the old woman said, she traced a picture of a flaming chalice in the sand with her finger. Then she wrote the motto underneath it. "It gave me the strength to live each day," she said. Whenever she drew the chalice in the dirt she was reminded that some day the world would remember the important truth that every single person is important and should be free to think and believe as he or she chooses.

When we see people light the chalice at the beginning of our service every Sunday, we can enjoy it because it is a lovely thing to do. But we can also remember the story of the flaming chalice and the strength it has given people for hundreds of years. We use it to let others know that Unitarian Universalists believe in helping others.

—NOREEN KIMBALL

The Minister Who Was a Scientist

Joseph Priestley's Search for Truth

Do you know what most people like best about drinks like Coca Cola or Sprite? They like the bubbles—the fizz. And it was a Unitarian minister in England, Joseph Priestley, who experimented with gases in his laboratory and made the very first fizzy drinks.

It's hard to imagine a minister messing around in a science lab. But that's just what Priestley did back in the mid-1700s. He was a curious person who asked lots of questions. He had questions about how things worked in the universe and he had questions about religion, too. To Priestley, the things that science taught us about the world and the things religion taught us about the world couldn't be separated from each other. Priestley thought they were both important and he could see that both were always changing as human beings had new experiences and new ideas.

This was a very different way of thinking, especially for a minister. In fact, in those days it was against the law to believe things that were different from what the Church of England taught people about religion. The Church of England taught that Jesus was the son of God and that all human beings are born sinful. But Priestley liked to study things when he had questions about them. He wasn't sure he believed that Jesus was the son of God so he studied the Bible. He decided that a person could believe that Jesus was a wonderful teacher without believing that he was the son of God who was sent to earth to save sinful people.

Joseph Priestley had lots of questions about animals and plants and gases, too. His questions led him to study and perform experiments that helped him to discover some important things about science that you learn in school today. He is considered the person who "discovered" oxygen.

It was pretty hard in those days to believe things that were different from what everybody else believed. The Unitarian churches where Priestley found work as a minister were always small and poor and they were often attacked by people who were afraid of his ideas.

For a few years, Priestley left church work and started his own school. In Priestley's school, students were taught to ask questions about everything and to work on their own ideas and experiments. His ideas about education, just like his ideas about religion, were very different from what was normal at the time. Although some people thought his teaching was very good, the school never made enough money to support his family, so it closed.

Finally, in 1773, Priestley got a job as a librarian and family tutor for the Earl of Shelbourne, a very wealthy man. The earl liked Priestley and gave him space and money to do his experiments. During his years with the earl's family, Priestley wrote many books about air, electricity, and even about drawing! In his writing, he always told the whole story of his experiments—the mistakes he made, as well as his successes. Priestley was more interested in finding the truth, in both religion and science, than in proving that his ideas were right.

When his job with the earl ended, Priestley took another job as minister, this time in a church where people agreed with his religious ideas. He was very happy there for about ten years, but the fighting between the traditional church leaders and the new ones got worse until finally, Priestley's house, church, library, and science laboratory were burned to the ground by an angry mob. Priestley and his wife barely escaped. Shortly after that they moved to the United States where Priestley's grown-up sons had already gone to start a new community in Pennsylvania.

The Priestleys settled in the small town of Northumberland, about a five-day trip from Philadelphia. It took four years for Priestley to build his house, and it was even longer before he had a scientific laboratory to work in again. During those years, Priestley traveled several times to Philadelphia to help set up a Unitarian congregation. The church wanted him to be their minister but he always returned to Northumberland. And although he never took a job as a Unitarian minister in the United States, we remember him as a founder of

Unitarianism in America because of his work with the Philadelphia church. Priestley spent the last years of his life doing experiments and writing about the history of Christianity. Science and religion were the two great interests in his life until he died in January 1804 at the age of seventy.

—BETSY HILL WILLIAMS

The Preacher, the Farmer, and the Little Church That Waited

The Life of John Murray

ohn Murray was born in England. His family, led by a stern father, rose at dawn each Sunday to spend the whole day praying and attending church. After church John's father would quiz him on the sermon. If John couldn't answer every question, his father would strike him with a cane or box his ears.

Sunday was a time to sit and think about hell—a place where the Murrays believed most people went after they died, and burned in flames forever and ever.

John's parents believed in the Calvinist idea of God—that God decided whether a person would go to heaven or hell before that person was even born, and a person could do nothing to change this. Furthermore, only a certain few people were chosen to go to heaven. The Murrays and others in their church thought that if you attended church a lot, and if you worked very hard, and if you were very good, and if you made a good living, it could mean that God had chosen you for heaven. That is why John's father was so strict.

John tried to please his father. At the age of six, he could read entire chapters of the Bible. He developed a talent for speaking and, as a teenager, he was often asked to preach in nearby churches.

When John was nineteen, he left for London and took a job at a cloth mill. But he was careful to attend church every evening and on Sunday, and he woke every morning at four o'clock to pray. He began to think that maybe he was one of the special few persons chosen by God to be saved. He started to feel and act superior to others.

Then one day in church John met Eliza, the most beautiful young woman he had ever seen. He immediately fell in love with her, and she fell in love with him. Soon after, John and Eliza married.

At this same time in London, a small group of people called Universalists were preaching ideas about God that were very different from the Calvinists. "John," said Eliza one day, "who are these Universalists?"

"I don't know," he answered. "I hear they are evil and dangerous people."

"What do they believe?" asked Eliza.

"From what I hear, they believe some crazy idea that . . . well, that every person will go to heaven because God is so good!" said John.

"To tell you the truth, John," said Eliza, "I sometimes wonder myself why a truly good God would want millions of humans to go to hell. Besides, John, is anyone really completely good?"

John felt uneasy. It seemed wrong to question what he had been taught all his life. "Let's find out more," said Eliza.

John and Eliza learned about the Universalist ideas about God. They spent several years carefully thinking through their beliefs. In the end, they chose Universalism.

Their friends were shocked and refused to be friends anymore. John and Eliza didn't care. Universalism gave them hope in place of stern judgment. John discovered that he no longer looked down on people. He now cared deeply about others, rich and poor. He and Eliza made new friends, and to add to their happiness, they had a baby boy.

Then suddenly everything changed. Their baby died and Eliza became sick. John spent all their money and borrowed more to save her, but she died. Then John was thrown into debtor's prison for owing money.

"I have come to pay your debts, John, and get you out of this place," said Eliza's brother who came to John's rescue. John replied, "My wife and my baby are dead. I don't care whether I live or die. Just leave me."

But Eliza's brother brought John home anyway. "Come on, John," said his friends. "Preach Universalism for us. We need you."

"I shall never preach again," John said, "but I know what I will do. I'm going to cross the ocean to America, and lose myself in the wilderness. I am done with the world."

In 1770, John sailed to America in the *Hand in Hand*. The ship was supposed to dock in New York City, but the captain miscalculated, and instead, the *Hand in Hand* got stuck on a sandbar off the coast of New Jersey. The captain asked John to go ashore to find fresh food and water for the crew.

John was glad to get off the ship and after walking some distance through the tall pines, he came to a clearing with a large house and, to his astonishment, a trim-looking church made of rough-sawed lumber. A tall farmer stood in front of the house cleaning fish.

"Welcome!" the farmer called out. "My name is Thomas Potter."

"And I am John Murray, from the ship *Hand in Hand*."

"Yes," said Thomas, "I saw your ship in the bay, stuck on the sandbar, she is."

"May I buy your fish to take back to the ship's crew?" asked John.

"You can have them for the taking, and gladly," answered Thomas, "and please come back to spend the night with my wife and me. I will tell you all about this little church and why it is here."

John gratefully carried the fish to the sailors, and then returned to Thomas's home for the night.

"Come, my friend, sit in front of our fire, this chilly fall evening," said Thomas. "I'm so glad you have come. You may be the very person I've been waiting for."

John wondered, "Waiting for! What could he be talking about?" Thomas explained.

"You see, I grew up here in these woods. I never had a chance to read or write, but I always liked hearing the Bible read, and I've thought a lot about religion. Trouble is, my ideas are different from the ideas of the preachers who travel through these parts. I built this little church myself for all the traveling preachers to use. I ask them questions and talk to them, but they don't know what to make of me and my ideas. I keep looking for a preacher of a very different stamp. I want a preacher who will teach about a loving God who saves all people, not just a chosen few. Today, when I saw your ship in the bay, a voice inside me seemed to say, "There, Potter, in that ship may be the preacher you have been so long expecting."

John said quickly, "I am not a preacher."

"But," said Thomas Potter, leaning forward, "can you say that you have never preached?"

"I have preached," answered John slowly, "and I believe, as you do, in a loving God."

"I knew it! I knew it!" shouted Thomas. "You are the preacher for whom I have waited for so long! You've got to preach in my church on Sunday!"

"No," replied John firmly. "I never want to preach again. Tomorrow, as soon as the wind changes, I will be on my way!"

After John went to bed, he couldn't sleep. He thought to himself as he tossed and turned, "I just want to get away from everything. If I preach Universalism I know there will be trouble. Folks here in America mostly have Calvinist views, just as in England. Why start trouble for myself in a new country? But Thomas Potter has such faith in me. And he's so kind. Oh, I wish I knew what to do."

By Saturday night the wind had still not changed, and John finally agreed to preach the next morning. Thomas Potter was overjoyed. He grabbed his coat and hat and ran for the door. "I'm going to spread the word to all the neighbors! They can expect a sermon such as they have never heard before!"

And so, on Sunday morning, September 30, 1770, Thomas Potter's dream came true and the first Universalist sermon was delivered in America. At last he could hear a preacher who talked of love instead of punishment.

As for John Murray, after that Sunday he knew he wanted to preach. Just as he expected, there were people who were angry at him for preaching ideas so different from Calvinism. They spread lies about him and stoned him, but he stuck to his beliefs and, in 1779, organized the first Universalist church in America in Gloucester, Massachusetts. After many years, he fell in love again and married. He and his wife, Judith, had a daughter and John Murray stayed in Gloucester. He helped to organize Universalism as a religion in the United States in 1793.

—CHARLENE BROTMAN, ANN FIELDS
AND BARBARA MARSHMAN

Meet Thomas Potter

The Man Who Built His Own Universalist Church

Every year, Nelson Simonson, a member of the Church of the Larger Fellowship, dresses up like Thomas Potter and visits Potter's church as part of a living history event. We couldn't go to the event but we called him on the phone and he agreed to answer some questions on Thomas Potter's behalf.

You are famous because you built a church on your land, even though you didn't have a minister. Why did you do that?

Potter: In those days, ministers traveled around the countryside preaching in different people's homes. They preached that God selected only a few of us to go to Heaven, and they said the rest of us would go to Hell. I didn't agree. I believe that God loves all people and would not make anyone suffer forever. My wife Mary and I kept searching for a minister who believed as we did. Mary got tired of having our house full of people every week, so I built a church on our farm.

Tell us about how you met John Murray.

Potter: It was late afternoon; I had finished my chores for the day and I was sitting outside with my dog. I saw this man walking down the road at about the same time he saw me. I knew, right then, that God had sent me a preacher. And I was right! John Murray had been a preacher in England who taught that God would surely save everyone—but people there did not agree with him. When his wife died, John Murray left England to start a new life in America. Mary fixed supper for us. After we ate, I showed John Murray my church and told him that the wind would not change, and therefore his boat could not depart, until he preached in my meetinghouse. I don't know how I knew this was true but I was so sure . . . and, I was right! On September 30, 1770, John Murray preached for us.

Did Murray stay with you?

Potter: John continued his journey to New York. But he came back and stayed with us for several months. When he was with us on Sundays, John would preach in my meetinghouse and it was overflowing. Later, he was called to Gloucester, Massachusetts, where he married Judith Sargent and preached until he died in 1815.

—BETSY HILL WILLIAMS

One Fine Day

The Story of the First Universalist Sermon in America

This foolish porridge must thicken soon! I've been stirring the pot well nigh an hour and my arm is like to fall into the fire. Still, if it sticks to the pot and burns, father and mother will pinch their lips together. They will not scold me, but I will not have so fine a day if I have made them sad. And I want a good day today. There be strangers in the town and there will be exciting things to hear and see.

Gideon comes in from feeding the chickens and he is jumping and howling, chasing the cat as usual. I shush him, but he will not pay me any mind. I'm only his big sister. I worry so about Gideon. No matter how mother clucks her tongue at him or how Father tries to tire him out with long walks and busy tasks, Gideon will always make noise. And a mess too. I catch him by the waist as he runs by again and he puts his rosy face up to me for a kiss. I give him a quick one on his cheek and settle him in his wooden high chair. I push it in to the table so he cannot squirm down. I give him an apple to keep him busy. He's torn his skirts again. I know boys don't begin to wear trousers until they're five years old, but I think Gideon would be safer in trousers than he is tripping around in skirts.

When the porridge is cooked, I open the wooden shutters on the window to let the sun in. Master Thomas Potter on the next farm has two windows with glass in them. Even on the coldest days, he and Mistress Potter have sunlight coming in to the house. If we could have glass in our windows, it would make me happier than almost anything I could think of. Except, of course, a church to go to—like everyone else.

While I wait for mother and father, I look at Gideon. He is munching on his apple and watching the bird through the window. Hetty Greene, who goes to the church in town, says Gideon's mischief-making is a sign that he is not saved—that he will go to hell. Father says I am not to worry about such things. But Hetty goes to church and we do not. Father says he will not let his family go to any church that frightens children. I understand, but it is hard to be the only ones who do not go.

The door opens and mother and father come in together. Mother fills our bowls with the porridge and father pours a glass of buttermilk for Gideon and for me. Father tells mother about the strangers who have come to our town. "The ship is called the *Hand in Hand*," he said, "and she was bound for New York until she got stuck on the sandbar out in Barnegat Bay. You know how bad the fog gets there. A man named John Murray came ashore to find food and water. He went to Master Potter. It seems this

Murray was a preacher back in England, and Thomas will have it that Master Murray must preach in his church."

"Thomas Potter will be so happy!" Mother said. "He built that church ten years ago, hoping to find a minister who believed as we do. Is Master Murray the one we have been waiting for?"

Father laughed at Gideon who was trying to sneak more honey onto his porridge. "We will see if he's the one. He told Thomas he could not preach because he and his ship had to leave as soon as the wind changed. Thomas said that the wind would not blow for the ship until Master Murray had preached in the church!"

"What?" said mother. "Is Thomas pretending to know what the wind will do?" she laughed.

"Well," said father, "if the wind does not change today, we will be off to church at Master Potter's farm in the morning. That is if Master Murray agrees."

All day, I found myself looking out the window to see if the leaves on the trees were moving. And they weren't! I helped mother to carry the carrots and the potatoes to the root cellar where they would keep in the dark until we needed them. I hung our quilts out on the bushes to air in the sun and I chopped onion and beans for soup. I saw mother peeking out the window too. Finally, as the sun began to set, mother said, "Abigail, I think we should take your calico and mine out of the chest and shake out the wrinkles. We might be needing those dresses for church tomorrow!"

A few minutes later, father came in from the haying. Mother and I watched patiently as he washed his hands and face at the bowl in the corner by the door. He sat by the fire and slowly filled his pipe with tobacco. Finally, mother said, "Jason! What is to happen?" "Well, Ellen," father said, "tomorrow we will hear a Universalist sermon in Thomas Potter's church. And I am ready for it. I am ready to hear a preacher who believes that all people are worthy to go to heaven. And I want our Abigail and our Gideon to hear this Universalist preacher too." In the morning, as father, mother, Gideon, and I walked the short road to Master Potter's church, I looked over to the Bay. There in the water, its sails very still, sat the ship. Father, mother, Gideon, and I had a church of our own to go to. A Universalist preacher come all the way from England would be our minister. And for once, I did not mind that there was no wind to cool us as we walked in the hot September sun.

—NOREEN KIMBALL

Angel of the Battlefield

*Clara Barton
and the American Red Cross*

ang on tight to the mane!" Clara heard her brother call as she galloped bareback across the field. Clara was only five years old, but already her older brothers and sisters had taught her to do more than most five-year-olds did—especially in 1826! She was the baby of the family, and she loved learning to read, spell, and do arithmetic. Clara lived with her family on a farm in North Oxford, Massachusetts.

Every Sunday, Clara's family drove five miles in a horse and carriage to the Universalist church. Clara's father had helped to build that church and Clara never forgot the Universalist teachings she learned there. She learned that God is love, and that all lives are precious gifts that should not be destroyed.

When her family was not with her, Clara was very shy. This worried her parents, so they sent her away to school when she was nine years old. They hoped she would make friends and forget to be shy. But Clara was so homesick she asked to come home.

When Clara was eleven, her brother David fell from the top of their new barn and was badly hurt. The doctor said he might die. "Please," begged Clara, "let me be David's nurse! I'll take very good care of him!" Her parents and the doctor agreed to let Clara try, so she stopped going to school. Clara stayed with David day and night. She fed him, gave him his medicine, and changed his bed. This was Clara's first job as a nurse and she did it cheerfully every day for two years!

When she was seventeen, Clara took her first job outside of home. She taught a class of forty children, from four years old to thirteen years old—all in one room! Clara heard that some of the boys liked to make trouble for the teacher, so on the first day at recess, she offered to play baseball with them. They were surprised to see that she could throw a ball just as hard as they could, and run just as fast! The boys felt a deep respect for their new teacher, and Clara never had to spank or hit her students with a ruler the way other teachers did in those days.

A few years later, a friend in Bordentown, New Jersey, asked Clara to start a public school. Some people there didn't like the idea of public schools that were free, but that didn't scare Clara away. It just made her feel even more sure that she wanted to start the public school. She offered to open a school for children of all ages and teach without any pay for three months. The school board agreed to give her an old building. On the first day, only six students came to class. But Clara was so popular and such a good teacher that soon there were six hundred children coming! The town built a new, eight-room schoolhouse. Clara wanted to be the principal of the new school, but in those days nobody would hire a woman to do that job. Instead, the townspeople asked Clara to be the "female assistant." Her pay would be only half the amount of money the town would pay a man to be the principal. Clara felt that this was unfair so she gave up teaching and moved to Washington, D.C., to find a new career.

Clara was living and working in Washington when the Civil War broke out. She saw that the soldiers who were coming home from the war were hungry and they needed clothes and bandages for their wounds. The government was not able to help so many soldiers. Clara saw what they needed, and she used her own money to buy food and clothes for the soldiers. She wrote to the newspapers and asked them to tell people what the soldiers needed. People gave blankets, medicines, and other supplies.

Then news came from the battlefields that medicine and food did not get to the soldiers. Wounded soldiers fell to the ground and lay there without food or water. Many died of thirst or cold because there was no one to take them to the army hospitals. There were no women nurses to help them. In those days people thought that women were not strong enough to take care of soldiers or be near a war! Seeing women on the firing line shocked the soldiers.

But Clara knew she must do exactly what most people thought no woman could do. At first the Army laughed at the idea, but Clara kept right on asking until she got permission to go to the front lines of the battle. With a wagon full of supplies pulled by four mules, she came to a battlefield in Virginia at midnight. The army doctor who was in charge was very tired and he had completely run out of supplies. Clara went to work cooking and taking care of the wounded right away. She even learned to take bullets out of wounded soldiers with a penknife! Later the army surgeon wrote, "If heaven ever sent out a holy angel, she must be the one!" After that, Clara was known as "The Angel of the Battlefield."

For fourteen battles, Clara brought supplies and took care of wounded soldiers from both sides, Confederate (South) and Union (North). She nursed anybody who needed help, because she still believed what she learned in her Universalist church when she was a child: that every life was precious. She said, "I have no enemies."

Once, she was kneeling beside an injured man, giving him water, when a bullet tore through the sleeve of her dress. It hit the man and killed him instantly. Another time she barely escaped from a battle by jumping onto a horse and then leaping from the horse onto a moving train!

When the war ended, eighty thousand men were missing from the Union armies. Every day, Clara would hear from women and children who wanted help to find their loved ones. President Abraham Lincoln asked Clara to come to the White House to help him work on this problem. Two weeks later, President Lincoln was shot and killed. Clara was working by herself again. With money President Lincoln gave her, and some of her own money, Clara set up an office. She asked prisoners and others who had been in the war about what had happened to the missing people. She wrote down what they told her and kept the information to help find the missing soldiers.

Soon the money ran out and Clara needed to raise more. Since there was no TV or radio in those days, people would buy tickets to hear speeches about what was happening in the country. Clara began to give lectures about what she had seen during the war. It was hard for Clara to speak in front of hundreds of people. She was still shy. "I would rather stand on the battlefield, than speak at a public meeting," she once said. But large crowds came to hear her wherever she went, and she was able to make enough money to keep her office going. After two years of public speaking, she lost her voice and had to quit.

Clara's doctor suggested she go to Europe to rest. In Geneva, Switzerland, Clara learned about a new organization called the International Red Cross. This organization was started to help soldiers in battle no matter whose side they were on. Clara went back to the United States and talked to the American lawmakers and asked them to join this organization. She wanted them to sign the Geneva Treaty. This treaty was a promise by all the countries who signed it. The promise meant that during a war, doctors and nurses could take care of the sick and wounded soldiers no matter what country they were from. It was not easy, but she finally convinced the lawmakers. In 1882, the United States became a member of the International Association of the Red Cross.

But Clara didn't stop there. She had an idea. Why should the Red Cross only help people during wars? Why not use the Red Cross to help people in all kinds of disasters like forest fires, floods, and earthquakes? She explained her idea to other countries, and many foreign leaders gave her medals for her work. Clara was president of the American Red Cross for twenty-three years and a Red Cross worker until she was eighty-three!

The next time you take Red Cross swimming lessons, learn Red Cross first aid, or read about the Red Cross coming to the rescue in some disaster, remember Clara. She was a shy but very brave young Universalist girl who grew up to start the American Red Cross!

—BETSY HILL WILLIAMS

Faith Is the Gift of God

How King John Sigismund Brought Peace to Transylvania

Four hundred years ago, there was a little country tucked in among the high mountains of Hungary called Transylvania, or "The Land Through the Forest." The King of that land was John Sigismund. Crowned king when he was only twenty-one years old, he was already brave and thoughtful—and he needed to be, for he and his little country had some *big* troubles.

King John's father died of an illness when King John was a baby, so he had to make his way without a father to guide him. As a boy, John was never very strong or healthy; he often felt dizzy and weak or had a stomachache, but he did not give in to these feelings any more than he could help. He learned to play all the sports that other young men at his court enjoyed, such as sword fighting, horseback riding, and deer hunting in the forest.

King John's country was right next to two large, powerful countries that fought with each other a lot. King John worried because he did not want his little country to get into their quarrel. But even worse than that—King John's own people often fought each other in "The Land Through the Forest." They fought because they belonged to four different kinds of churches. The churches were Roman Catholic, Lutheran, Calvinist, and Unitarian. The people in each church said, "Our ideas about God, and Jesus, and what a church should be like, are the only true ideas. Everyone," they thought, "should believe what our church tells them to believe." People only wanted to believe in the teachings of their own church.

Sometimes the people fought with words—arguing and saying the worst things they could think of about each other, whether they were true or not. Other times, the church that had members in government fought by taking people's jobs away, or people's money. Often people were put in prison or even put to death. When times were at their worst, people even tried to kill King John himself, because they hoped a new king might make their church the one, true church. Actually, this kind of fighting about churches happened in a lot of countries in that part of the world.

King John thought for a long time and then he made a decision. He called the best speaker from each church to come to a place called Torda for a debate instead of a fight. A debate is an argument with rules: each person takes a turn to speak about his or her ideas. There is no quarreling because only one person speaks at a time. A judge decides who has the best ideas. The debate began each day at five in the morning and it lasted ten days.

The speaker from the Unitarian church was a man named Francis David. He argued that no one has the right to force people to believe anything about God.

After ten days, King John ordered the debate to end. But he did not announce a winner; he did not say that any of the four churches was the best. This probably surprised many people. King John did listen to the argument of Francis David though, that no one should be forced to believe in any religion but should be able to choose for himself or herself. Then, King John made an important announcement that was called the *Edict of Torda*. The edict told the people that from that time on, his subjects could debate about their ideas of religion, but they must not fight, punish, or kill each other about religion. Every church and every person would be free to follow their own beliefs. This was a new and strange idea for those times, and many people were angry with King John for this law, but he stuck to it. Unitarians especially remember King John because his law made it safe for them to be Unitarians.

—HEATHER B. McDONALD

When you hear the name *Transylvania*, you probably think of the vampire, Count Dracula. Dracula is from a famous story by Bram Stoker. Though *Dracula* is just a story, there really is a place called Transylvania and there really was a person named Dracula. Vlad Tepes Dracula III ruled Wallachia, a little country near Transylvania, nearly six hundred years ago. The history books say the real Dracula used to kill people who disagreed with him, and when soldiers chased him, he escaped to Transylvania and lived in a castle there. This may be why Bram Stoker named the vampire in his story Dracula.

Our story of Transylvania starts in the 1500s, when King John Sigismund was the ruler. He passed a law that let people in his country follow whatever religion they found most true. One of the religions that grew strong under this law was the Unitarian religion. Sadly, the peaceful

Partners in Transylvania

Unitarian Universalist Churches Connect Across an Ocean

years of King Sigismund did not last long, and the little country of Transylvania suffered a lot of wars during the next 400 years.

Transylvania is a piece of high, flat land in the Carpathian Mountains. Like other small countries around it, Transylvania has had many different rulers and has even been part of different countries over the years. At the end of World War I, in 1918, the whole area of Transylvania became part of the country of Romania, and the people of Transylvania enjoyed a time of peace. Some American Unitarians set up the "sister church program" to help replace the bells in the Unitarian churches in Transylvania that had been melted down for bullets during the war. Sadly, these peaceful years did not last long either.

All the countries around the Carpathian mountains were forced into World War II (1940-1945), and at the end of the war, many were taken over by the powerful United Soviet Socialist Republic (USSR). For the next forty-five years, the people had a communist government like the one the USSR had—and they were not free. The people were not able to communicate with their sister churches in America and many Unitarian churches became run-down.

Ten years ago, a group of people from the Unitarian Universalist Association in Boston, Massachusetts, visited communist Romania to show support for Unitarian churches. The Americans arrived one week *after* the communist government lost all its power. When the American visitors returned to the United States, they decided to bring back the sister church program, and to call it the Partner Church Program.

Today about two hundred North American Partner Churches are paired with a Transylvanian, Hungarian, or Czech Partner Church. The children and youth of the two congregations send photos and videos and letters back and forth so they can "meet" each other and learn about how their lives and their churches are different. Sometimes the young people make very exciting visits to each other—traveling almost halfway around the world to meet one another in person and share their lives for a few weeks.

—BETSY HILL WILLIAMS

Here They Come!

A Visit to Transylvania

Hello. My name is Bettje and when you say it, it sounds like "Bet-tay." I live in Transylvania, in the village of Kadacs where my grandfather, Biro Josef, is the Unitarian minister. We say our last names first here, and then our given name—or what you call a first name. My mother teaches first grade in the same school that I go to. For the last three weeks, she has been teaching me and my friends a song in English called "My Bonnie Lies Over the Ocean." We learned it so we could sing it for some American visitors who are coming to our village today.

One of our visitors is a lady minister from our Partner Church in America. I've never seen a lady minister before. I didn't know there was such a thing. My grandmother, Biro Anna, has been writing letters to her for over four years. They are pen pals. She has sent things for the people in our village from the people in her village of

Norwell, in Massachusetts. And she has been selling some of our folk art embroideries and beautiful tablecloths made by women in my village in America. The money from those embroideries really helps us.

We have enough to eat because we all have gardens and most of us keep pigs and chickens. Everyone works in the garden. Almost nobody has cars. We walk everywhere. It's hard in the winter and spring because it's so muddy, and the roads in our village are not paved.

Anyway, today is the day. We have all been practicing our English song. Everybody has been doing something for the visit. The ladies have been cooking all week. The men have been repairing the fences and the beautiful carved gates called *szekley kapu* that many people in the village have outside their houses. The teenagers have been practicing the folk dances of the village so they can perform them. We don't get to see them except at weddings and times like this. People are beginning to forget how to do the folk dances. The grandparents remember, but there are so few of them left.

Unfortunately, today is also the day that the sheep are driven out to pasture for the summer, and they are going to leave a lot of "stuff" on the road as they go. My grandmother is worried that the visitors, especially the lady minister and her husband, will think our village looks this way all the time.

Here they come! I can see the van and I can see hands waving out the windows. I wonder which lady is the minister? The van is stopping and they are getting out. Lots of people are coming out of their houses to see and greet them. They don't look that much different than us. Oh, that must be the lady minister, she and my grandmother are hugging each other and crying and another man is taking their picture. Wow, there are flashing lights everywhere!

The man taking pictures of the lady minister is her husband and back in America he has a garden that he loves. He spends many hours each week in that garden making all kinds of things grow. Anyone who has a garden knows that you need more than water and sun to make things grow well, you must have fertilizer. And some of the best fertilizer in the world is the "stuff" that farm animals drop wherever they go. The lady minister's husband saw the sheep droppings in the road and explained that he doesn't live on a farm so he has to pay for fertilizer for his garden. He thought it must be wonderful to live in a farming village with so much free fertilizer on the road for anyone to take. Well, I guess that's one way of looking at it. It sure cheered up the people at my grandmother and grandfather's house who were worrying that the visitors would think our town was a mess!

The Americans stayed five days, and the lady minister was actually speaking some Hungarian words by the end of the visit. Her husband looked at all the gardens in the village, but he only learned one word, *Palinka*. That's a grown-up drink. I think it tastes awful, but like many other things, I guess it depends on how you look at it. I hope they come back. The lady minister said she'd write to me . . . in Hungarian!

—JUDITH C. CAMPBELL

Tales of Yesterday and Today

The Water Bearer's Garden

A water bearer in India had two large pots, each hung on one end of a pole that he carried across his neck. One of the pots had a crack in it. At the end of the long walk from the stream to the master's house, the cracked pot arrived only half full, while the other pot was perfect and always delivered a full portion of water. For two years this went on daily, with the bearer delivering only one and a half pots full of water to his master's house.

Of course, the perfect pot was proud of its accomplishments, perfect to the end for which it was made. But the poor cracked pot was ashamed of its own imperfection, and miserable that it was able to accomplish only half of what it had been made to do. After two years of what it perceived to be bitter failure, it spoke to the water bearer one day by the stream. "I am ashamed of myself, and I want to apologize to you."

"Why?" asked the bearer, "What are you ashamed of?"

"I have been able, for these past two years, to deliver only half my load because this crack in my side causes water to leak out all the way back to your master's house. Because of my flaws, you have to do all of this work, and you don't get full value from your efforts," the pot said.

The water bearer felt sorry for the cracked pot, and in his compassion he said, "As we return to the master's house I want you to notice the beautiful flowers along the path."

Indeed, as they went up the hill, the old cracked pot took notice of the sun warming the beautiful wild flowers on the side of the path, and this cheered it some. But at the end of the trail, it still felt sad because it had leaked out half its load, and so again the pot apologized to the bearer for its failure.

The bearer said to the pot, "Did you notice that there were flowers only on your side of the path, but not on the other pot's side? That's because I have always known about your flaw, and I took advantage of it. I planted flower seeds on your side of the path, and every day while we walk back from the stream, you've watered them. For two years I have been able to pick beautiful flowers to decorate my master's table. Without you being just the way you are, he would not have this beauty to grace his house."

We all have our own unique flaws. We are all cracked pots. In God's great web of life, nothing goes to waste. Don't be afraid of your flaws. Acknowledge them, and you too can be the cause of beauty. Know that in our weakness we find our strength.

—ANONYMOUS

The Floating Bridge of Heaven

In the far-off beginning, the air and the earth, the land and the water were mixed up together like an egg white and yolk scrambled up for cooking. Within this scrambled-egg world was a tiny seed of life, which grew slowly through the ages. Finally, the seed grew enough to cause the great mass to stir, until at last the top of the great egg rose and became the sky. The bottom of the egg settled down and became a muddy ocean. Up in the sky there appeared fleecy clouds. A rainbow bridge of misty-colored light stretched down from the sky to the heavy ocean of mud. From out of the muddy ocean a green sprout started to grow. It grew higher and higher until it was a green stalk and it reached the fleecy clouds. Then the green stalk wished a big wish. It wished to grow into a god, and behold, the great wonder came to pass—the tall green stalk grew into a god.

But the new god felt lonely. He wished for friends. So he made other gods to keep him company. He made a great many gods and they all lived together on the fleecy clouds.

The most adventurous of all these many gods were the last two gods to be born. One was Izanagi (i-za-na-ge), a boy god; and the other was Izanami (i-za-na-me), a girl god.

One time Izanagi and Izanami were walking together along the Floating Bridge of Heaven. Looking down, they began to wonder what was below them. So Izanagi, taking his jeweled stick, stuck it down deep into the muddy ocean below and stirred the waters. As he lifted his stick out of the water, some lumps of earth stuck to it and then fell back into the ocean. As the lumps touched the surface, they began to harden like the white of an egg hardens when it is cooked. The lumps grew and came together and they became the first land upon the earth—one of the islands of Japan.

Izanagi and Izanami stepped down from the Floating Bridge of Heaven onto this island that Izanagi had made. They started to walk around the island, going in opposite directions to explore it. When they met again they were glad to see each other. Izanagi said, "What joy beyond compare to see a maid so fair!" So Izanagi and Izanami fell in love with each other and became husband and wife.

Then the two of them made even more wonders come to pass. They made other islands rise out of the muddy waters. Eight large islands they created. They made grasses, bushes, brooks, rivers, lakes, and mountains. They covered the hills with forests; they placed snow upon the tops of the mountains and made flowers grow on the plains.

Then Izanagi and Izanami looked out over the beautiful floating islands that they had made and said, "We have made the beautiful eight-island country with its valleys and rivers, forests and mountains. Now we need sons and daughters to rule over these lands!" Because they were gods, their wishes came true.

Their first child was a very beautiful daughter whom they named Amaterasu (a-ma-ter-a-su)—Heavenly Light—because her face shone with a glorious brightness. "She is too beautiful to stay down here," her parents said. "Her light should be where she can shine on all the children who may be born upon these islands," thought Izanagi and Izanami. So they sent their first daughter up the ladder that reached high in the sky, and placed her high above the earth where, as the Sun Goddess, her light still shines on everyone.

Their next child was also a lovely daughter whose light was a soft silvery kind—and her face shone with a shimmering brightness that was most beautiful. They called this daughter Tsuki-yumi (soo-ke-yu-me). Izanagi and Izanami sent Tsuki-yumi also up the ladder into the sky, and there, as the Moon Goddess, she still shines on everyone.

The third child born to Izanagi and Izanami was a son whom they named Sosano-wo (so-sa-no-wo). This new child grew to be a very stormy god, and he liked to make people upset and angry. His face was dark and gloomy. Izanagi and Izanami were afraid that Sosano-wo might hurt the beautiful islands they had made, so they commanded him to stay always on the ocean. But Sosano-wo still caused trouble. When he was angry he would not only blow great storms over the ocean but he would also come up on land, and with his hot breath, he would blow down the trees of the forest and kill the flowers and rice plants that his sister Amaterasu had made to grow by shining her sunlight on them.

One day Sosano-wo secretly climbed up the ladder to the sky to play a trick on his sister, the Sun Goddess. She was sitting in the great weaving hall of the gods and was weaving beautiful robes out of the rainbow's mist. Sosano-wo climbed up on the roof of the clouds, made a hole in them, and threw a big lump of mud down at Amaterasu's feet. This was not the first time Sosano-wo had caused problems for Amaterasu. But this time she was so angry that she decided to hide from her mean brother. Gathering up her shining robes, she crept down the ladder of heaven to the earth and entered a cave. Rolling a stone to block the entrance to the cave, she hid herself from of all the gods. Suddenly the earth and the sky became dark, and all the gods were very much troubled.

Everyone agreed that they couldn't go on without Amaterasu. So, they made a plan to get the Sun Goddess to come out of the cave. All eight million gods and goddesses on the earth and in the sky gathered at the cave in which Amaterasu was hiding. They brought trees and set them up in front of the cave. They hung jewels and swords and lovely new robes and scarves upon the trees. They lit a bonfire before the cave, and one of the best dancers began to dance a very merry dance, while others played on harps and drums. The music and dance was so merry that the eight million gods and goddesses began laughing and skipping, shaking the earth with their noise. At last the sound of this great party made the Sun Goddess curious. She went to the entrance of the cave. She pulled back the big stone a tiny bit and peeped out. No sooner had she done this than one of the powerful gods outside pushed the stone away and pulled a laughing Amaterasu out of the cave.

Amaterasu's anger softened when she saw how much everyone loved her and wanted her light to shine. The other gods carried her up the ladder into the sky and once again the earth and sky were light.

A joyful shout rose from the earth.

Never again, since this long-ago time, has the Sun Goddess left the sky except to rest for the night while her sister, the Moon Goddess, sheds her soft light upon the earth.

As the ages passed, many gods and goddesses were born to the great Sun Goddess. One son became a mortal man, the first great ruler of the eight-island empire. From that day to this, all the emperors who ever ruled Japan have been related to the first son of Amaterasu, the beautiful Goddess of the Sun.

—SOPHIA LYON FAHS
AND DOROTHY T. SPOERL

She was bewildered. Bewildered and ashamed. The other hands in the classroom were smooth with nails cleanly cut. Hands raised to answer the teacher's question. Hands engaged in the age-old art of spit-ball forming. Hands writing on the blackboard. They all seemed so new, so unused, so beautiful.

May hid her hands. In kindergarten she hid them under the table. In first grade she hid them under the desk. In second grade, third grade, and even fourth grade, she hid her hands in this way. Winters were always easier, thanks to grandma's homemade mittens. Colorful and bold, decorated with baby ducks and, later, with purple and blue stripes, the mittens meant May felt no shame walking to school carrying books and lunch for herself and her sister.

Exclamations like, "Oh, how beautiful," and "I wish my grandma would make some mittens with stripes," stirred up hope inside

Beautiful Hands

May, and for a brief moment she would tell herself she was one of them, for they would forget her hands and remember, instead, her beautiful mittens.

Back in the classroom, May would catch someone looking in her direction and shove her hands back under the desk. She never raised her hand, never applauded with excitement. She wrote in hurried strokes of the pencil so as not to have her hands in full view for very long.

One day she was walking through the school hallway, with her hands shoved into her pants pockets. In the hallway that day, she saw a poster for an art class. It was a special art class, it was going to be taught by her favorite teacher, and each student was going to be able to learn how to draw and paint. She signed her name on the poster and all the way home, she thought about what kind of art project she might make. Her mom worked all night long while she watched her younger sister, and she thought maybe her mom would like a pretty picture to look at when she got home from work. She also thought about how tired mom was during the day, trying to sleep while the rest of the world was awake, and May thought she might make a "Do-not-disturb!" sign for the front door. And then she remembered her beautiful mittens, and thought she might draw a pattern to send to grandma so grandma could make new mittens, even some for her sister.

As soon as May got home, she sat her sister, Kate, at the kitchen table for a snack. As she did the breakfast dishes and tried to keep Kate quiet so they would not wake up Mom, May thought of all the wonderful art projects she could try. May was so busy planning her project, she forgot about her hands. She finished the dishes, got out the mop to clean up the milk that didn't quite make it to Kate's mouth, and chopped potatoes for dinner. Mom was up by now, and was rushing out the door to get to work. Mom kissed May on the head, told the girls she loved them so-o-o-o much, and went off to work.

May helped Kate with her bath, tucked her into bed, made up mom's bed, and vacuumed the front room. After doing her homework, May went to bed and dreamt of being a famous artist. Everyone in town marveled at her beautiful paintings, she won awards from her school, and even got to give a speech in front of the governor.

When May woke up, she jumped out of bed, excited about the art class. As she braided Kate's hair, she saw her hands and suddenly realized she could not paint or draw without the other children seeing her hands.

She could not get Kate ready fast enough, and practically pulled her all the way to school. May ran to the hallway to cross her name off the poster. It was not there. The poster and sign-up sheet were gone. She went to class and told her teacher she needed to drop out of the art class. The teacher said she would have to go to the art class and tell the art teacher that she was no longer interested in the class.

When May went to art class that day, she tried to get the teacher's attention, but there were so many other children in the class and such a lot of noise that May decided she would wait until after class to talk to the art teacher.

After the teacher got the class to quiet down, she talked a little bit about drawing things, how important it was to draw what you saw, even if no one else saw the same thing. She said they would eventually draw their pets and maybe even a family member, but that their first lesson was to draw their own hand. May was stunned, and tried her very best not to cry in front of the other children. Though there were many things she wanted to draw, her hand was certainly not one of them. Still, she did her best though she was ashamed to even look at the rough redness around her nails. She had little bumps on her palms, and the lines in her hands reminded her of grandma's hands. May finished her drawing and left as quickly as possible, even before the teacher had collected the hand pictures and told them what they would be doing the next day.

The following morning, May determined to tell the art teacher she could not take the class anymore. When she got to art class, the teacher talked about all the wonderful hand drawings she had gathered from their desks the day before. The art teacher laughed about the hand drawing that showed pink- and purple-dotted fingernails. She laughed about the hand that had diamond rings on every finger, and four diamond rings on the thumb. Then she held up a hand drawing that was familiar to May. It showed a small hand, with fingers curled toward the palm as if holding a precious stone or delicate butterfly. May shoved her hands under her desk, and wanted to crawl under there to hide along with her hands.

The teacher said, "Of all the hand drawings I saw yesterday, this is the one I could not stop looking at. This is an interesting drawing, a beautiful drawing, for it shows a hand that is not idle. It shows a hand that has worked hard. The fingers are curved, as if to protect something fragile." She walked to May's desk, and asked May, "Could I please see your hand?" May did not want to show her hand, but being accustomed to obeying teachers, she pulled her hand out from under the desk. The teacher took May's hand into her own.

"Now," said the teacher, "as I hold in my own hand the hand from this drawing, I can see that I was not wrong. It is a hand that has caressed little kittens and held small daisies. It is a hand that has washed many dishes, folded laundry, given baths, and combed hair. Yes, this is a very interesting hand. It is a beautiful hand."

With that, the teacher went back to her desk and started talking about that afternoon's drawing assignment.

After class, May ran all the way home, dragging Kate part of the way, and carrying her the rest of the way. She put the drawing on Mom's bed, and with her rough red hands, she washed the dishes, fixed dinner, bathed Kate, and finished her homework. As she lay down in bed, she noticed that the glow from the moon was shining on her hands. They looked different tonight.

May thought of the many dishes and counters she washed when Mom was sleeping. She thought of the times she had bathed her sister and cleaned up the house when Mom was at work. She thought about the way her palm fit over Kate's cheek, and how wonderful her sister's soft skin felt to her hand. She remembered the tender kisses Mommy gave her hands when she came home from work in the dark hours of the early morning. She would hear her mommy say, "Thank you, May, for all your help. I could not do this without you."

Just as the little girl with the red, rough hands was starting to nod off, she looked one more time at her hands. And she smiled, for they really were most interesting hands.

—BARB PITMAN

The Buddy Thing

very September Ms. Ryan worried about the new kids who would be in her fifth grade class. She knew how hard it was to be new—her family moved a lot and by the time she finished sixth grade, she had been to four different schools. So, every year Ms. Ryan tried to help new kids by picking someone in her class to be their "buddy," to show them around, sit with them at lunch, and include them at recess.

This year the new kid was a boy named Matt. Matt was from a really small town and everything about his new home in the city was different. The kids he met over the summer seemed older and smarter than his friends back home. They all had computers or Nintendo in their own bedrooms, and it seemed that everyone had been on some kind of winning sports team at school. Matt didn't like sports that much and his parents couldn't afford Nintendo.

Ms. Ryan picked Alex to be Matt's buddy the first week of school. Alex was a popular kid and Matt felt lucky to hang out with him. Unfortunately, Alex didn't feel the same way. Fact was, Matt was pretty different: he used expressions no one ever heard before, his hair was cut like Alex's had been back in third grade, and he looked like he was dressed up for Sunday School every day. Alex was embarrassed being with him all the time, and as the weeks passed, he used every excuse he could think of to get out of being Matt's buddy.

"Alex," asked Ms. Ryan one day, "Can you help me move these bookshelves before lunch today?"

"Sure," agreed Alex, wondering what Ms. Ryan *really* wanted.

Alex was right. Ms. Ryan was just looking for an excuse to talk with him. "Alex," she started, "I notice that you are avoiding Matt these days. What's up?"

"I don't know," stammered Alex, feeling bad that he hadn't been a better buddy for Matt. "I guess we're just not friends, that's all," he replied defensively.

Ms. Ryan saw Alex's discomfort. "Look," she said, "I know it's hard for you to include Matt in your circle of friends. Probably just as hard as it is for Matt in some ways. It's okay if you don't want to be his buddy anymore. You tried, and I thank you."

Alex headed out to recess surprised that Ms. Ryan had been so understanding and nice about the buddy thing. "She always says she cares about all her students— I guess she really does," Alex thought to himself. He felt bad that it hadn't worked out with Matt, but mostly he was relieved that he didn't have to hang out with him anymore.

Out of the corner of his eye, Alex caught Matt standing in the middle of a group of boys in the outfield.

"You can't hit and you can't catch! Why are you playing with us anyway?" he heard one of them yell.

"Yeah," chimed in the other boy, "If you have to play, go out in right field, *way* out, okay?"

Matt was quiet as he turned to leave the field. Suddenly Alex felt Ms. Ryan's kindness and caring for *him* well up inside for Matt. Ms. Ryan had accepted him and forgiven him for not wanting to be Matt's buddy. Nobody should be made to feel bad for just being the way they are—including Matt.

"Hey, Matt," Alex said as he caught up with him. "I heard what those guys said. You know, if they were better ball players themselves, they wouldn't care about how you play. They just hate to lose—poor sports."

"Gee, I hadn't thought of it like that," replied Matt. "But I know how they feel. I don't like to lose either, and I'm always messing up. Guess that's why I don't like sports."

"What do you like to do?" Alex asked.

"Mostly I like making stuff. I have a ton of Legos and car models and stuff like that. My dad said he'd get me a kit to make my own Go-Kart if I saved up for half of it."

"That's cool," said Alex, "The Go-Karts are my favorite ride at Canopy Lake Park."

"What's that?" asked Matt.

"Oh, it's a cool amusement park not far from here," answered Alex. "Maybe my mom could call your mom and we could go there sometime."

"That'd be great," answered Matt. "And thanks, Alex. I know everyone around here thinks I'm kinda weird. And I guess I am different from you guys." He paused for a minute, "But if you think I'm weird, just wait till you meet my little brother!"

"You too?" laughed Alex, "He can't be worse than mine! C'mon, we'd better run or we'll be late and I want to talk to Ms. Ryan before class starts."

—BETSY HILL WILLIAMS

Don't Smash Santa

The piñata was shaped like Santa Claus, with a red suit and white beard. Molly loved Santa Claus. Some of the kids at kindergarten had been teasing her because she believed in Santa Claus, but Molly didn't care. Santa was real to Molly.

Molly stood admiring the piñata as it hung from the top of the doorway between the living room and the kitchen. She liked the tree her father called the "solstice shrub," and her grandmother's menorah, but she liked the new Santa piñata best. It was just for her.

Molly could smell the cookies her mom was baking and hear her brother, Isaac, rummaging around in his closet.

"Got it!" he cried, and burst into the room with his Star Wars light saber. "I couldn't find the plastic baseball bat but this'll work."

He shoved it into Molly's hands and said, "Go for it, girl." She looked at him, puzzled.

"Go for what?"

"Smash the piñata!"

Molly tried to give back the light saber. "I don't want to smash it!"

"But that's what it's for. Go ahead! Smash it!" Isaac insisted.

"It's okay, Mol," her dad added.

"But I don't *want* to." Her chin started to crinkle. Why was Isaac being so mean?

Her mother ducked under the Santa and knelt down next to Molly. "That is what it's for, honey. It's a Mexican tradition. Piñatas are full of candy. When you break them, the candy showers down and you get to eat it . . . well, not all at once, of course."

Molly still did not want to smash Santa.

"Wonder what kind of candy it's got?" Isaac said. "Hurry up, kiddo!"

Molly's mom went back in the kitchen, looking back over her shoulder encouragingly. "Go on, lovey."

"But I like Santa. I don't want to break him."

"Just *do* it!" Isaac shouted.

Molly took a good grip and swung the light saber. She missed completely.

Dad said, "Try again, Mol."

Molly swung again and this time sent the piñata dancing on the end of its string. It danced so hard that Molly missed it on her next swing.

"Wait till it stops, slugger," said Isaac, getting impatient.

Molly gave him a glare. She was getting red in the face and her stomach didn't feel good. She turned back to the piñata and poured all her upset into a powerful swat.

The piñata burst.

But nothing fell out of it. Santa was smashed and there was no candy. Molly picked up a big piece of Santa's belly and cried.

"What a gyp!" Isaac said. Molly didn't hear him, or her father's reminder that their family didn't use words like *gyp*. She was sobbing bitterly.

"You made me ruin it and there isn't even any candy, and you said there would be candy!"

Molly's mother sat down on the floor and Molly crawled into her lap, cradling the piece of Santa. Her dad unrolled a curl of paper glued to the top of the piñata.

"It says, 'Fill with candy,' dear."

Molly's mother made a face. "Oh, Molly. I really blew it." She rocked Molly and stroked her hair.

Gradually, Molly stopped wailing. Eventually, only her wet cheeks and hiccups showed how upset she had been. Isaac unhooked the remains of Santa. The buzzer on the stove went off and Molly's mom struggled to her feet, still holding Molly. She perched Molly on the edge of the counter and pulled two cookie sheets out of the oven.

"When these are cool, we'll have some."

The cookies smelled wonderful. Molly's dad put milk and glasses on the kitchen table. He lifted Molly down and gave her a little push toward her chair.

"Isaac! Want warm cookies?" he called.

"In a minute!" Isaac called from his bedroom.

"I think I just learned something, Molly," her mother said. "In fact I think we all learned more than one something."

"What?" Molly's voice was strange. She cleared her throat.

"Well, first off, I learned to read the directions."

Molly's dad felt the cookies and put four of them on a plate. "Spit-sizzling hot!" he said. He always said that. "Isaac! Cookies!"

"Coming!" Isaac came into the kitchen, but he didn't sit down at the table. He picked something up off the counter and disappeared again.

"Be right back."

"What else did we learn?" Molly wanted to know.

"What else did we learn?" Molly's mom turned the question back to Molly.

Molly thought about it. "I learned . . . that I like Santa better than candy. Especially when there isn't any. And that getting mad makes you do things you don't want to."

"I learned that respecting peoples' feelings is more important than traditions," Molly's dad said.

"I wonder if Isaac learned that too," Molly's mom muttered.

"Learned what?" Isaac asked. He was holding something behind his back.

"That respecting people's feelings is more important than traditions," Molly's dad repeated.

"Sounds right," Isaac said around a mouthful of cookie. "I learned something else, too."

"What?" asked Molly.

"That you can fix a piñata with duct tape," Isaac crowed, pulling the almost-as-good-as-new Santa from behind his back and swinging it in front of Molly.

"Watch the milk!" Molly's mom grabbed Molly's teetering glass, but Molly never noticed. She was smiling at Santa.

"You can put him on your dresser," Isaac suggested.

Santa was the last thing Molly saw before she went to sleep, not just that night, but on many nights in many Decembers to come. Nobody ever put any candy inside, and nobody ever again smashed Molly's Santa piñata.

—VALERIE WHITE

A Pretty Good Day After All

There I was, coming home from school on the bus. I figured, it had been a pretty good day, one of those days when nothing much had gone wrong. As far as I knew, I was doing fine, and I was feeling pretty good.

So I looked across to the other side of the bus, and there was Genevieve Figuereto, who was in my class, and I gave her a smile. No big deal; she's okay—for a girl—and I was feeling good, so I smiled at her.

And she didn't smile back.

She just looked at me like, "Who are you, and what are you smiling at me for, goofball?"

I thought, "I wonder what I did wrong?" And I didn't feel quite so good any more.

But still, I felt good enough to wave at my neighbor, Mrs. Quackenbush, who was out in her front lawn raking leaves. Mrs. Qackenbush liked it when I waved at her, because her own grandson lived pretty far away, like in Ohio or someplace, and she always gave me a big wave back.

But that day, she didn't.

She didn't wave back. She just looked like, "Who are you? And what are you waving at me for, pinhead?"

"Hmmm," I thought. "I wonder what I did wrong?" And I really didn't feel all that good any more.

But still, I felt good enough to smile when I saw my dog, Ginger, lying on the front lawn, and I shouted, "Hey, Ginger!" Ginger was always glad to see me and would spring up on all fours and wiggle her behind and bark a time or two and then run across the lawn and try to jump up high enough to lick my face.

Except that day, when she sort of looked over at me, without getting up, like, "Who are you, and what are you yelling at me for, dumbo?"

"Wow," I thought. "I don't know what I did wrong, but it must have been something awful." It was getting pretty hard to remember that I felt good.

So I didn't have all that big a smile left for my father when I walked in the house. "Hi Dad," I said, and started to go off to my room.

"Hey there, hotshot," he said. "Why the sad face? Something go wrong today?"

"Well," I said, "I really messed up, and I feel pretty bad."

"Some days are like that," he said. "I'm sorry. Do you want to talk about it?"

"Sure," I said, but then I couldn't remember right away what it was I had messed up so bad. But I could remember that Ginger knew what it was.

"Ginger didn't even run to see me when I got home, that's how bad I messed up today," I said.

Dad said, "Oh, Ken, that's not you, that's just the way she's been today. Something she ate, your mother figures. At least she's finally lifting her head. Maybe she'd even like a walk. Why don't you take her?"

So I did, and you know dogs, the chance for a walk perked her right up, and the next thing you know, about the time we got to Mrs. Quackenbush's house, she was trying to jump high enough to lick my face.

That made me giggle, which made Mrs. Quackenbush look up from her raking again and this time she smiled. "How did you get home without me seeing you?" she asked. "I must have been busy thinking about that rude new person at the supermarket," and she made a face like she thought he was a pinhead. It wasn't me after all.

So I was feeling better, and I gave her a big wave as Ginger and I went off, and she gave me a big wave back, you know, the way that she does.

I bet you think that next I ran into Genevieve Figuereto. I bet you think along she came on her bike, cheery as can be, and stopped and talked to me, like I wasn't a goofball at all. Well, it's true, that's what happened.

So I asked her real friendly how she was, and she said fine, now that her dentist appointment was over, the one she had right after school. She said she was pretty worried she was going to have a cavity, but she didn't.

She said it had turned out to be a pretty good day for her after all. And I said, yeah, it had turned out to be a pretty good day for me, too, and I was feeling pretty good.

Lots of the time, you just don't know what's going on inside other people's heads, and lots of the time—not all the time, but lots of the time—when they look worried or bothered or sore, what's on their minds isn't *you*.

—KENNETH SAWYER

Raychel and Tony

Tony had always been good at art, but he didn't always get good grades. His teacher told his parents, "Tony is talented but he doesn't follow directions."

"Well," said Tony to himself, "that doesn't make sense to me. People who make art are supposed to follow their own directions—not someone else's." But the teacher didn't seem to agree with him, so Tony kept his thoughts to himself. And he began keeping his artwork to himself too. Sometimes, he would do what he was supposed to do for the class and then he would do it over again at home, the way he wanted to do it. But he wouldn't show anyone those drawings.

One day, the art teacher asked the class to do their "self-portraits," a picture of yourself that you drew yourself. The teacher said they could use anything they wanted to use to make the picture. She told them to look in a mirror so their picture

Courage to Create

would really look like them. Tony was not interested. He knew he could make a picture that looked just like himself—he had practiced drawing himself lots of times. When he asked if he could do something different, his teacher asked him to do the same assignment as the rest of the class.

Tony began to think about how he would do his self-portrait and what he would use. "Hey," said Tony to himself, "I'll use all the art supplies I have. That will at least make the picture more interesting." And he began to feel better about the project.

That night after supper, Tony borrowed a mirror from his mother and propped it up on some books so he could see himself. Then he got out *every* kind of art supply he owned. He got out lead pencils, and colored pencils, and charcoal, and colored chalk, and watercolor, and glue, and his old "cutting-up" magazines, and scissors, and brushes, and piled them all up on the floor beside his work table. Then he tried to get started. But he just couldn't keep his mind on his face and what he was supposed to be drawing. His eyes kept wandering to all the other things he could see in that mirror: his sports equipment, his posters, his model cars, his old stuffed animal, the quilt his grandma made him when he was adopted, his old sneakers, half a sandwich, the cat, his fishing rod. There was so much stuff in that room, it was getting in the way of his "self-portrait!"

Tony looked again into the mirror and suddenly he saw that all the stuff he could see in the mirror *was* his self-portrait. The things in his room were all of the things he liked best. Now Tony was really excited—he knew how he would do his self-portrait. He would draw himself, just as he was supposed to, but he would draw himself with all the things in his room. This self-portrait would be much better than just a picture of his face.

It was past Tony's bedtime when his mother come upstairs and found Tony still happily at work.

"Tony," said his mom, "that is wonderful. Wait till your teacher sees it, she'll be amazed."

"She won't see it," said Tony. "She won't like it. I didn't do it the way she said to, so I'm not going to bring it to school. I'll do it the right way over the weekend. It's not due until next Monday."

"I don't understand," said his mother. "This is beautiful. I would know it was all about you even if I didn't see your face peeking out through everything. Why wouldn't your teacher love it?"

"You know how the teacher is always telling me to follow directions? Well, I tried but the picture just kind of took over. She said just to draw our face the way we saw it in the mirror. But I think all this other stuff is part of me so I made it part of my self-portrait. I really like it. It's ok, I'll do the picture her way in time for school."

"Well I don't think this is okay," said his mom. "You just made something really wonderful and you don't think you can bring it to school?"

"Yup," said Tony.

Tony's mother sighed. "It's time for bed now, Honey. Let's talk more about this tomorrow."

The next day, Raychel came home from school with Tony. So it was the two cousins and Tony's mom who sat down at the kitchen table to try and sort things out.

Tony's mom began. "Tony has made a picture that he—and we—really like. He put a lot of time into it, and he had a lot of fun doing it. But he's so sure the teacher won't like it that he's going to hide it in his closet and not share it with anyone. I, for one, feel very sad about that and would like to help Tony figure out another way."

"I'm just tired of Ms. Epstein and all the other kids putting me down cause I like to do things my own way."

"Some kids are just bursting with ideas and they have to let them out," replied Tony's mom.

"But why don't other people like that?" Tony wondered out loud.

"That's a hard question," began his mom.

"I think they're jealous," Raychel chimed in. "They wish they had so many ideas. At least I do."

"You may be right in some cases, Raychel," replied Tony's mom. "But mostly I think people just say things without thinking of others' feelings. It takes courage to be creative. First, you don't know what other people are going to think of your idea or work. And then they often respond to it without thinking of your feelings. I can see why creative people get discouraged sometimes. I wonder if your teacher really knows how you feel about art, Tony?"

"I have an idea," said Raychel. "How about this? Tony, don't do another picture yet. Take this one in to your teacher and show it to her and tell her this is what came out when you did your homework. Tell her what happened. Then tell her that you are willing to do another one her way if that's what she wants. Just tell her that you wanted her to see the picture you really like before you started another one. See what she says."

"Good idea, Raychel," said Tony's mom. "That's sounds fair to the teacher and to Tony, too."

The following Monday, Tony wrapped up his self-portrait and took it to school. He explained to his art teacher that it was a little different than she expected. He told her that he almost didn't bring it in but his parents and his cousin really liked it—he really liked it, too. He told her that he wanted her to see it but that he would do another one, following her directions, if she wanted him to.

The teacher looked at Tony's self-portrait for a long time. Tony was sure she didn't like it.

"Tony," said the teacher, "this is a wonderful self-portrait. It is very different, but it says so much about you. It doesn't just show what you look like. It shows what is inside you and what is around you, too. I'd like to enter your self-portrait in the annual scholastic art exhibit. I think you might win a prize."

"You mean I don't have to do it over again?" asked Tony.

"No," said the teacher, "I'm the one with the homework this time."

"What do you mean?" asked Tony.

"Tony, you are a very creative boy. I've known that since the beginning of the year. I'm sorry you haven't been very interested in what we do in class. Even very creative people need to learn how to use the tools of their art and how to do assignments and exercises that will help them get better. But now that I see what good ideas you have, I can see I need to give you more choices about how you make your art. We need to get you ready for art school someday."

"Wow," said Tony.

"Wow and wow again," said his teacher, "I'll get this piece framed for you and get it to the show. You better get moving, you're late for your next class!"

"Wow," said Tony. "Thank you, Mrs. Epstein."

"Thank you, Tony."

—JUDITH C. CAMPBELL

Free to Believe

Hey Dad," called Raychel, "is it okay if I go over to Heather's house for dinner tonight?"

"Didn't you go over there twice already this week, honey?"

"But tonight is special. There's a meeting of a club from Heather's church called the Handmaidens. She asked me to join. They play games and go on camping trips and they do good stuff like helping poor people. She said there are some things club members have to believe and some things they have to promise to do—but it's no big deal. I think it sounds cool."

"Wait a minute here, my dear." Raychel's dad liked rhyming words when he could. "What church is Handmaidens connected to? You already have a church."

"I don't know much about the church," said Raychel. "All I know is that they have a girls' group called the Handmaidens and a boys' group called the Soldiers. Heather's brother, John

Peter, has asked Tony to join that one. Sometimes the two groups do things together. It sounds really neat."

"I think we should know more about what you are supposed to believe and what you are supposed to do to be a member of this club before you decide to join," said her dad.

"But Dad," argued Raychel, "we're Unitarian Universalists. Didn't you tell us we're free to believe anything we want? What if I decide to believe the things the Handmaidens believe? That's okay isn't it?"

"It might be okay, but only after you have done a lot of hard thinking about it. Unitarian Universalists don't just believe anything. We ask lots of questions and make sure that the beliefs—and the things people do because of them—are things that make this world a better place," explained Raychel's dad.

"Tell you what though, you go to your friend's tonight and tomorrow we'll all talk about it. Then, if you still want to, you can join them."

The next day, Tony and his parents joined Raychel's family for dinner. At the dinner table, as usual, everybody was talking at once. Raychel's dad, Val, stood up and banged his spoon on the table to get everyone's attention. In a big, booming voice he said, "Hear ye, hear ye, the dining table will come to order."

"Raychel Morgan, will you tell us about your visit to the Handmaidens?"

"It was boring," sighed Raychel. "First they read from the Bible, and everyone recited the Handmaiden's Creed, which was all about obedience to authority and the leaders—whoever they are. Then we played a game with words from the Bible. Heather's mother talked to us about how important it was to be a Handmaiden and how we had to try and get more kids to be Handmaidens so more people would get the message and be saved. I wanted to ask, 'What message?' and, 'Saved from what?' but nobody else was asking questions. Anyway, I didn't like it."

"Sounds a little different from our church," said Raychel's dad.

"It was really different from our church and our youth group," Raychel continued. "But when they asked me about our church I couldn't think of anything to say. They knew exactly what to say about their church and what they believed. But what do Unitarian Universalists believe?"

"Raychel has asked a very important question," said her dad, "Can anyone sitting here give answer to that question?" He was having fun talking like a real judge.

"Well, what about the words we say at the beginning of church," Tony offered. "You know: 'Love is the doctrine of this church, the quest for truth is its sacrament and service is its prayer . . .'?"

"I can say the words, but I don't get what they mean," said Raychel.

"Those words are a perfect place to begin," said Raychel's father. "We believe that love is the strongest power in the world—stronger than hate and stronger than fear. I like to call this power God, because that's the best word I know for a power that is so much bigger and stronger than any person. Your mom doesn't like to use the word God, because it makes her think of an old man sitting up on a cloud. But even though she doesn't use the same word to describe this power of love, she believes in it the same way I do. And 'doctrine' simply means something that is taught. So the first line means that we teach love."

"What about the next line, 'the quest for truth is its sacrament'? What does that mean?" asked Raychel.

"Well," continued Raychel's dad, "a sacrament is an object or an act that is considered very, very special in a religion. Other words used to describe these things are 'sacred' or 'holy.' A quest is a journey to find something. So the second line means that we consider searching for truth to be a very special and important part of our religion. And to us, searching for truth means more than never telling a lie."

"Like what?" asked Raychel, getting confused again.

"For one thing, it means that what might be true for us today might not be true tomorrow if we learn something new."

"You mean like when people used to think the world was flat until someone noticed it was really round?" asked Tony.

"Or that only birds could fly until someone invented an airplane?" added Raychel.

"That's it," answered Raychel's dad.

"Or that someone named God invented the world in seven days even though the study of science has given us different facts to believe," added Raychel's mom. "You see, some people believe that God told the truth many years ago to men who then wrote it down in a book like the Hebrew or Christian Bible or the Islamic holy book, the Koran. They believe that this one truth is the only truth they need to know to live a good life. So they don't question it."

"Other people, like Unitarian Universalists," she continued, "keep asking questions because we believe there is always more to know, always new ways of thinking and acting that can make the world a better place."

"So what does 'and service is our prayer' mean?" asked Raychel. "How can service be a prayer?"

"Most Unitarian Universalists believe words alone aren't enough. We have to work to make a better world, not just talk about it," said Raychel's mom.

And for a moment, strange as it seems, everybody in this noisy wonderful family was quiet.

"So," said Raychel's dad, "what do you think?"

"I still think Unitarian Universalism is a hard religion to explain," answered Raychel. "But from now on, when I'm asked, I'm going to say, 'We believe in love, we believe in searching for truth, and we believe in making the world a better place.'"

"I think that's a very good answer Raychel," said her dad. "It says a lot about how we think in just a few words. And in this family, saying anything in just a few words is amazing indeed!"

"So, Raychel," said her dad, "do you think you'll be joining the Handmaidens next week?"

"Well," said Raychel, "I think I ask too many questions to make a good handmaiden."

—JUDITH C. CAMPBELL

aychel was really scared. Today was the day she had to go into the store at the mall and steal something. Some of the kids at school had formed a club, and if you wanted to be a member, you had to steal something. Raychel wanted to be a member of the club.

Today was Raychel's turn. She hadn't slept well at all the night before, and when she did, she had awful dreams. Her mother knew something was wrong, and had asked to talk about it. Raychel said she just had a little stomachache. She wanted more than anything to tell her mother why she didn't feel good. But she knew she could never say to her mother, "Hey mom, guess what, today I'm going down to the mall and steal something." But now that the day had come, she didn't know which she felt more: afraid or ashamed. She was afraid she'd get caught, and she was ashamed of being afraid

One of Us

when the other kids didn't seem to be. But mostly, she was ashamed that it meant so much to her to belong to the club that she would actually go and steal something just to be in it.

Her mother and father said that she should always think for herself and not follow the crowd. Well, what did they know? They had their friends, lots of them. How would they feel if the only way they could have friends or belong to a club was if they had to do something like this? They'd do it in a minute.

All these thoughts were tumbling around in Raychel's head as she got on the bus. She couldn't pretend to be sick again, she did that the last time it was her turn to do the stealing. She really wanted to run away, but she didn't know where to go.

All day in school, thoughts like these were roaring around in her head. The teacher even spoke sharply to her, telling her to stop daydreaming, and pay attention to what was going on in class. "She should only know what I'm daydreaming about," thought Raychel, "I could go to jail!"

The school day went faster than any Raych remembered. Amy was snickering at her, and even sent her a note that read "only two more hours, and you'll be one of us."

Raychel went to the bathroom about ten times that day. Even the teacher asked if there was something wrong.

"No," said Raych, "I just drank too much milk at lunch."

Raychel had to get permission from her mother to be let off at the mall, so that no one would be worried when she didn't come home at the usual time. The note said that one of her parents would pick her up later that day.

At the mall, Raychel decided she would steal a scarf. Her heart was pounding so loudly she couldn't hear anything and her knees and hands were shaking as she walked to the scarf counter. She started looking at them like she was going to buy one. She looked around, just as she had seen Amy do, then she quickly rolled a scarf up in a ball and stuffed it in her pocket and hurried out the door.

"I did it," Raychel thought with a sigh. Then she felt someone take her arm and turn her around, asking, "Would you like to show us what you have in your pocket?" Raychel realized then that the very worst thing that could possibly happen had just happened. She was so scared, she wet her pants.

The rest of the afternoon was a blur. It was a blur because Raychel was crying so hard. When she stopped crying enough so that she could talk, she poured out the whole story without stopping. Without telling anyone's name, she told about the club, and about being afraid, about wanting friends, about how she didn't want to do it and had chickened out once before, and how her parents were going to be really mad.

"We do have to call your parents," said the detective, "and they will have to come and get you. We are not going to press charges. We have the scarf, and I don't think you will ever do this kind of thing again."

It was a few more minutes before Raychel's mother came through the door. At the sight of her, Raychel started crying all over again. All she could say was "Mummy, I'm sorry, I really didn't want to do it."

Raychel's mother introduced herself to the two detectives, and thanked them for calling her. Then she turned to Raychel. "You have a lot of explaining to do young lady. And you can forget about going to the mall on your own again."

"Well," said the detective, "officially, Raychel can forget about the mall for a year. That's what we do when we have a first-time offender, and we don't think that person will steal again. You won't do it again, will you Raychel?" the detective asked.

Raychel just shook her head from side to side.

"Come on Raych," said her mother, "we have some talking to do."

"Before you go Raychel," said the store detective, "why don't you see if you can get those other kids to come and return the stuff they have taken? We won't press charges on them either."

The ride home was very quiet. Both Raych and her mom needed time to think about what had happened and what they would do next.

Raychel's dad was furious. And he was also upset with the girls who had made stealing the way to get into their group. He wanted to call their parents at once and tell them what had happened.

"I know what," said Raych, "why don't we give them a chance to do the right thing? Tomorrow, in school, I'll tell them exactly what happened, and what the detective said. Then they can decide whether to return the stuff, or risk getting in trouble."

"That certainly puts the responsibility right where it belongs," said her dad. "Good thinking Raych. But their parents may still need to be involved. I'll ask the mall detectives to let us know what happens, and we'll see if I need to call their parents or not."

"Dad, am I really grounded?" asked Raychel.

"You most certainly are," said her dad. "What you did was wrong. Stealing is wrong no matter why you do it. You did it knowing it was wrong, but you decided that belonging to the club was more important to you. I don't think you'll ever forget today, but being grounded will help you remember it even more."

"How long?"

"How long do you think?"

"A month?"

"That's probably right, but we'll have to ask your Mom what she thinks, Raychel," said her dad. "We love you. We don't like what you did, but we will always love you. Can you understand that?"

"Yes, I do," said Raychel . . . and she really did.

—JUDITH C. CAMPBELL

Everybody thought Tony was happy about moving up to middle school this year, but he really wasn't. He tried to pretend he was happy and excited; he even teased his cousin Raychel. She would still be going to elementary school when he moved to the big regional middle school across town. But Tony was really terrified.

Everything at middle school would be new. He wouldn't know most of the kids. Sure, his whole class was going, too, but they'd all be in different classes. After six years of going to school with the same kids, he had to start all over. Some of those middle school kids were *huge*!

He remembered his visit to the school last year. Some kids wore pants so baggy they dragged on the ground, and other kids were dressed all in black. He didn't even know what he should wear on that first day. What if he wore the wrong thing and the kids made fun of him? What if he

Starting Over

got lost and the kids made fun of him or a teacher yelled at him?

And the worst part was, he didn't dare tell anybody. His parents had always told him that if something was bothering him he should talk about it. He wished he could talk to someone about it, but how could he tell anybody he was scared of going to school? So scared, in fact, that he was having bad dreams about it. And it wasn't just the new school—he didn't want to ride the bus, either. The middle school was way across town, and the ride was almost forty minutes. A lot could happen to a kid on a bus in forty minutes.

Tony had to do something, and he had to do it fast. If he had thought about this sooner, he could have failed all his courses last year. Then he wouldn't have been promoted. Now, he had to go . . . or did he? Just then, an idea came to Tony, but he would need help. He decided to go to his cousin Raychel's house. He was always able to talk to her, and he would ask her to help him.

When he got there, Raychel was getting her new school clothes out for the tenth time that week. She was trying to decide what to wear for the first day. "Hi Tony," she said as she opened the door, "come on in. Want something to eat?"

"No thanks, Raych," said Tony, "I'm not hungry. What are you doing? What's with the clothes all over the sofa?"

"I'm looking over my new school clothes. I'm trying to decide which outfit to wear on the first day. What are you going to wear?"

"Cheez, Raych," said Tony, "guys don't think about what they're going to wear, they just wear whatever they pick up first."

"No sir," said Raych, "you should have seen all the guys at the store when I went with my mom. They pretended they were bored, but they tried on as many pants and shirts as I did . . . and you should have seen them in the shoe store! Picky, picky, picky. . . ."

"You must be really excited," Raychel said. "Middle school is so cool. You get to move around to different classes and meet new kids. The middle school even has dances. I can't wait. One more year and I'll be up there with you. My friend Julie's older brother started there last year. She says he's having a blast. She also said it was scary for him at first. That's hard to believe though 'cause it seems like such a cool place and Zak doesn't seem like the kind of kid to be scared. Still, Julie said he really was."

"Raychel," Tony said, interrupting her, "listen to me! I can't go to that middle school. I just know I'm going to get lost, or kids are going to stare at me or tease me cause I'm so short. I just can't do it, and I need your help. Next week, on the first day, I'll leave at the regular time. But instead of going to the bus, I'll hide in the bushes. Then when your parents go to work, I'll hang out in your garage for the day. I'll go home when the bus is supposed to drop me off. No one will ever know."

"You can't do that," sputtered Raychel. "What will you do all day? You have to go to school. Kids go to school. They have to!"

"Not this kid," said Tony. "I've heard stories about the way they pick on kids at that school, and I'm just not going."

"Tony," said Raychel a little more gently this time, because she was beginning to understand what was happening, "Tony, lots of kids are scared the first day. Do you think you'll be the only kid who doesn't know his way around? I bet lots of new kids feel smaller than everyone else. Remember the first day in elementary school? I was scared, but people showed me where to go when I got lost. They didn't make fun of me."

"You're a girl," said Tony. "Boys are supposed to know their way around. Asking questions is wimpy."

"Well, how are you supposed to know something if nobody tells you or shows you?" said Raychel. And then a great big smile spread across Raychel's face. "Tony," she said, "I have a great idea! Remember what I told you about my friend Julie's brother Zak? Well, Julie's coming over here tomorrow. What if I asked her to bring Zak with her and while Julie and I are figuring out what we're going to wear next week, he could tell you all about the middle school?"

Tony thought for a moment. "Maybe, but don't tell him I don't want to go or anything, just that I . . . well . . . just want to know what kids wear and stuff. You know, so I won't look different or anything," Tony said.

"I'll call Julie and Zak right now," said Raychel, "I hope he's home."

The next day, Julie and Zak came over. Raychel and Julie tore upstairs to decide about their clothes. Tony was pretending to watch TV. When Zak came in and sat down, Tony turned and looked at him. Raych was right. He did have really thick eyeglasses, and he had very curly red hair. In fact, Zak's hair was just like his, only Zak's was bright orange-red and he was even shorter than Tony!

"So, you're the one who's going to start middle school next week? I'm Zak, Julie's big little brother. I say big-little because I'm older than her, but she's already taller than me. I take after my dad. He's short too, but he's cool. He plays jazz saxophone.

"Middle school's OK, you know. I kind of kept my head down that first week. I thought the kids would pick on me, and I guess they did look at me kinda funny and laugh sometimes. But, so what, it happens to everybody and I just acted like I didn't hear it. They stopped after they heard me play the old piano in the cafeteria."

"Let's face it," Zak said, "you can spot this hair from a mile off. I used to hate it. I thought about wearing a hat over it the first day. But, what the heck, it's hair . . . my dad's losing his and tells me I'm lucky that I got so much."

Tony smiled in spite of himself. This guy talked as much and as fast as his cousin Raychel! Maybe Raychel was right after all. Maybe this Zak kid could help. "What bus do you take?" Tony asked. "And what are the kids like? Are they mean?"

Zak laughed. "I take the same bus as you. Some of the kids are nice and some are jerks. The teachers are OK, and changing classes is fun. You get a chance to move around. I used to go nuts sitting in the same chair all day long. And, like I said before, the kids picked on me for awhile because of the hair and the glasses. They stopped, though, when they found out it didn't make any difference to me. I still can play the piano with or without red hair and glasses. Do you play music?"

"No," said Tony, "but I am good at art, and I'm a good runner."

"I've never been very good at sports," said Zak. "It's always been music."

"So . . . what do the kids wear in middle school?" Tony asked.

"You name it," said Zak. "Different kids wear different stuff. There's the baggy pants guys, and the guys with black jackets. Some guys have tattoos, and some wear lots of chains and bracelets. And then there are all the kids who just wear regular clothes . . . I don't know. What do you usually wear?"

"I like jeans and tee shirts with crazy designs on them. Sometimes I make my own. Like I said, I'm good at art."

"You can paint tee shirts?" said Zak. "That's cool. Every year there's a contest for the school tee shirt. I'll bet you could do something for it. The art rooms are really cool; they've got tons of stuff, like potter's wheels and kilns."

Middle school was beginning to sound a little better. "So Zak," said Tony, "if I meet you at the bus stop, you think we could sit together and maybe you could show me where to go when we get to the school?"

"Sure," said Zak, "on the first day, there'll be some kids wearing special tee shirts showing the new kids where to go and answering questions. But definitely you can sit with me on the bus, and you can meet some of my friends."

Just then, Julie and Raychel burst into the room. "And what have you two been talking about?" asked Julie.

Zak looked at Tony and said, "Oh we were just talking about what to wear on our first day of school . . . it's a guy thing!"

—JUDITH C. CAMPBELL

All You Had to Do Was Ask

Tony felt terrible. Some kids had started playing basketball just for fun after school and he hadn't been asked to join one of the teams. He decided to go to his cousin Raychel's house to talk to her about it. Whenever something was bothering either one of them, they knew the best thing to do was to talk to someone about it. And for Raychel and Tony, that "someone" was each other.

"So," began Raychel, "why do you think they didn't ask you?"

"I don't think," said Tony, "I know they didn't ask me because they think I'm too short to play basketball, and because I like art. They think people who are good in art can't be good at sports. It's so unfair."

"They should have at least asked you if you wanted to try," said Raychel. "Then they would have seen that you run fast, faster than anyone I know. Being short and fast is good, you can run *under* those big guys and they would never even see you!"

"Thanks Raych," said Tony, grinning at the thought of running under and between the legs of the tall guys on the team. "You're right, they should have asked, but they didn't."

"This is just like the time I wanted to play football last year with the kids in the neighborhood," said Raychel. "They wouldn't let me even try because I'm a girl. They just assumed a girl is not strong enough or fast enough to play football. It made me so mad that they didn't even ask."

"What did you do?" asked Tony.

"Nothing. I just felt mad about it for a long time. I wish I had done something."

Just then Raychel's mom came into the room. "You know what?" she said, "I heard you talking and I had something like that happen to me just the other day. It turns out that the church down the street is looking for help with their food bank and they've been calling everyone in the neighborhood, except those of us who belong to a different church. Where you go to church doesn't matter if there are hungry people that need help! But they assumed that because I went to a different church, I wouldn't want to work with them."

"What did you do?" asked Tony.

"Well, I went to the church and found the person in charge and told him how I felt. He said right out he didn't think I would be interested in working for another church. I told him I was and that I have a big van that would carry lots of food and maybe even some other people from our church to help too."

"What did he say?" asked Raychel.

"What do you think he said?" her mother asked.

"I bet he felt really silly for not asking you," said Tony.

"Actually," said Raychel's mom, "he didn't say anything for a minute, and then he told me that he was sorry that he had made a wrong assumption. He was really glad I'd come and he asked me to help them this weekend."

"I don't know if those guys who didn't ask me to be on the basketball team would be so glad if I told them I can run," said Tony. "But I'm gonna tell them anyway. They probably won't get it that they made a wrong assumption about me until they see me in action."

"Well, that should work," said Raychel.

"Why do people do that, anyway?" asked Tony. "Why do they think things about other people and never bother to ask?"

"Well, we all do it," said Raychel's mom, "because we all think we know. We just don't realize how often we're wrong. And when people do it to us, it takes courage to change their assumptions. There is something we all can do . . . ." she started to say.

"We know, we know," said Raychel and Tony almost together. "Never assume anything about another person. Always ask first," said Tony.

"And when somebody assumes something about you that isn't true, I'll tell you just what you should do," said Raychel, who was like her dad and liked to make up rhymes on the spot. "When someone assumes something that just isn't true," Raychel began again, "then the work is up to you, to let them know just what is so, and in the end. . . ." Raychel paused looking for the last line of her poem.

"You can be friends," said Tony.

"Say that again," said Raychel's mother. "I think I know a few people who need to hear that!"

—J UDITH C. C AMPBELL

The Quilt That Love Built

Raychel and Tony were having a hard time thinking up what to do for their church service project this year.

"I want to do something really different this time—like the project where we sent a cow to Africa—that was so cool!" said Tony.

"I know what you mean," Raychel agreed. "Collecting bottles and cans and cleaning up the park were okay, but I want to do something that really makes a difference to someone."

They were sitting together on the big sofa in the family room, the one with the patchwork quilt that Raychel's grandmother had made for the family when they moved into their new home. She had put pieces of all of their old clothing and tee shirts into that quilt. Every square in the quilt held a little piece of the family history. Raychel was smoothing the quilt with her hands and Tony was sitting half under it when an "ah ha!" look appeared on Raychel's face.

"Tony!" she squealed, "we can all make a quilt and send it to the Women and Children's shelter. You know, the one where your parents help out? They're always collecting stuff like clothes and blankets. Each kid in our class could make a patch, and then after you and I sew it together, everyone could help with the quilting part. It would be just like the old-fashioned quilting bees I read about in school last year."

"Geez," groaned Tony, "I don't know. Guys don't sew!"

"You're good at art," said Rachel, "and who says guys don't sew? If I can hammer, you can sew."

Tony knew he was going to lose this argument. The quilt idea was a good one, and of course he could sew, he just didn't think he would like it. But then, he'd never tried it before.

"How will we get all the pieces?" he asked.

"We'll start by asking people who like to sew to make a patchwork patch that is exactly twelve inches square. If they don't have the cloth and needles and stuff to sew with, kids can just decorate a twelve-inch plain square piece of cloth with markers. We'll collect the squares and then my mother can sew them all together on the sewing machine. Then we'll take it back to church and after we add the stuffing and the backing, we'll do the final quilting all together, just as they did in the old days—only we'll have pizza and ice cream and . . . "

"Waaaiiiit a minute," said Tony, "you're going way too fast. What's the difference between a patchwork square and a plain square, and what's 'stuffing' and 'backing' and where to do we get all this stuff?"

"You're a pair of squares yourselves," joked Raychel's mother, as she joined the two. "I heard you from the kitchen, and I would be glad to help with this. I think it's a great idea."

"Raychel has a whole plan already," said Tony, "and I can't even figure out where to start!"

"I think you should start by measuring and cutting squares out of the cloth in our scrap bag. If you want me to, I could teach the kids how to make an easy nine-patch square," Raychel's mom offered. "Then, after we collect the squares, I'll sew them together, and show you all how to finish the quilt."

"Thanks, Mom," said Raychel. "This will be the best project ever. Do you think we could find out who gets the quilt at the shelter?"

"I don't know. Maybe they'll let us take a picture of the quilt and the person who receives it. What do you think?"

"I think we should go get your scrap bag," said Tony.

"But, I thought you didn't want to sew," teased Raychel.

"Well, maybe this once," said Tony grinning. "Besides, I can do lots of things if I think it's going to help someone else. That's the best part. So, where's the scrap bag and scissors? Let's get started."

—JUDITH C. CAMPBELL

Raychel's mind was racing as she and her cousin Tony loaded their sleeping bags and camping gear into her uncle's car. Camping in the state park was a real treat for Raychel. Her parents weren't big on sleeping on the ground in a tent but her aunt and uncle loved it, and often invited her along.

Tony had a zillion ideas about things to do that weekend and chattering with Raychel about them helped pass the hour it took to get to the campground. After the tent was up, the cousins and Tony's parents roasted hot dogs on sticks over the fire. Hot dogs and s'mores—that's what they had every first night of a camping trip.

"Raych?" Tony whispered after "lights out." "Can you hear me? I've got another idea for tomorrow."

"What's that?" answered Raychel.

"There's an old cabin somewhere in this park, and a strange old hermit lives in it. Let's go find it and see what he looks like."

Truth or Consequences

Raych sat up. "Isn't that dangerous?" she said. "What will you tell your parents?"

"We'll just tell them we want to take a map-walk like we did the last time, remember? We know how to read maps, the worst that can happen is that we see some weird old man, and we run back here before he catches us!"

"How do you know he's weird?" asked Raych.

"That's what the other kids said, so he must be."

The next morning, Tony's mom and dad invited them to go fishing, but Raych and Tony asked if they could take a map-walk instead. "Sure, use my pack to carry stuff," suggested Tony's mom. They packed water and granola bars, the map, and the help-whistle. "As if we'll ever need that," mumbled Tony, as he stuck it in the pack. Raych always carried hers, and soon she was going to be very glad she did.

The cousins followed the map to the very center of the park, where they found a little path going off to the left by a big stone. The path was overgrown, but clearly used, and the two kept following the flattened grass until they found an old cabin. They stopped, wondering what to do next. Tony picked up a rock and threw it yelling, "Hey old man . . . come out!" A huge dog, chained in the tall grass, leaped up barking and jumping at the noise. When he quieted down to a whine, Raych whispered, "That poor dog is so skinny I can see his bones."

Then they heard another sound from inside the cabin. It was a call for help.

"What are we going to do?" said Tony.

"How should I know?" snapped Raych. "This was your dumb idea. You figure it out."

"Aw, Raych," said Tony, "somebody needs help, and we're the only ones here. what are we going to do?"

"Blow the help-whistle," said Raych. "Your parents will hear it and they will come and find us and then we can get help."

"If we blow the help-whistle, they'll know that we told a lie and we'll get in trouble."

"So what?" replied Raych. "I'd rather get punished than leave someone crying for help."

They both heard the cry for help again, only this time the words were clear, "Help me . . . I'm hurt." Raychel and Tony didn't wait any longer, they both blew as hard as they could, then again . . . and again. One long blast, a short one and another long one. That was the "SOS" signal which means send help fast.

Tony's mom and dad were just reeling in a big trout when they heard the whistles. They dropped their rods and ran. The whistle meant only one thing, the children were in trouble. In a few minutes Tony's mom and dad burst into the clearing.

"Dad, Ma, there's an old man in there and he's calling for help and the dog won't let us near the house. You have to do something!" exclaimed Tony. His mom and dad were already moving carefully toward the house.

The dog wasn't barking now, he just lay with his head on the ground. They pushed in the door of the cabin and there they found the old man. He had fallen on the floor. It looked like his leg was hurt. "Hold steady old fella," said Tony's dad softly. "We'll help you."

They agreed that Tony and his dad would go and get help, and Raych and her aunt would wait with Sam, the old man. He wasn't scary at all; he was hurt and frightened. Sam told them he had lived in the woods for many years, talking to the birds and the raccoons and the skunks, and feeding them what little food he had to spare.

Tony and his dad returned with two police officers who would take Sam to a hospital where they could fix his leg. Tony's dad would take the dog until Sam was better.

When everything was settled, the four of them started back to the campground. It was then that Tony's dad asked the question that Raychel and Tony knew was coming.

"Would either of you like to tell us how you ended up at Sam's cabin when you told us you were going on a map-walk?"

"We didn't exactly lie, we just didn't say where we were going," Tony answered.

"Son," said his dad, "you can tell a lie with words, or you can tell a lie by leaving out the truth. That's what you did, and I'm not happy about it. You need to think about what you tell people and what you want them to hear, and make sure it's the same thing."

"It was my fault, too," added Raychel. "I went along with it and I didn't say anything either. I'm sorry."

"Yeah, me too," said Tony.

"You did do one thing right," added Tony's mom, "and that was blowing the whistle for help, even though you knew it meant we'd find out you lied. I'm proud of you for choosing to help a stranger, and getting help to do it."

"Sam seems like such a regular person," Tony remarked. "I thought he was going to be really scary and weird."

"Yeah," added Raych. "I'm sorry we didn't tell the truth about where we were going, but I'm not sorry we met Sam. Now we can go back to school and tell those other kids that they're wrong about him."

"It's easy to make mistakes about people if you only listen to the things other people say about them and don't take the time to find out for yourself, isn't it?" remarked Tony's dad. "Now let's get back to our campsite. There's a fish out in that river with my name on it!"

—JUDITH C. CAMPBELL

Two for One Summer

Andy was the name taped to the last empty bunk in the cabin. Tony unpacked his stuff and wondered what his bunkmate this year was going to be like. For the past two summers Tony had earned a scholarship to go to Walden, an art and theatre summer camp, because of his outstanding artwork in school. Last year his bunkmate, Drew, was a painter and they'd really hit it off.

"Hey, you must be Andy," Tony called out as a tall kid dressed in a heavy jacket walked into the cabin.

"Yeah, I am," answered Andy. "Sorry I'm late."

"I'm done with my stuff," said Tony. "Want me to help you make your bunk?"

"I can do it myself," snapped Andy. "I don't need any help!"

"Well, exc-u-u-u-u-se me," said Tony. "I was just asking. I didn't mean to make you mad or anything."

"Gee, I'm sorry," said Andy right away.

"I'm just tired of people feeling sorry for me and always trying to help me."

"What's to feel sorry about?" asked Tony.

"Tell me you don't notice anything different about me," said Andy.

"Well, you have a pretty heavy jacket on for July, but that's about all I can see that's different."

"It's this," said Andy, as he started to unzip his jacket. "I was born with only half of my arm so I don't have a left hand. There's a little nub that might have been a thumb or something at the end of it. I can move it a little. See?"

Tony wasn't sure he wanted to see. He'd never seen that kind of thing before and he was afraid he might say something wrong, or look grossed-out. But before he could do anything, Andy took off his jacket and pulled up his sleeve.

"Look," said Andy wiggling the little nub at Tony, "it's waving at you."

There was something about that moment—maybe it was because Tony felt so uncomfortable. Whatever it was, Tony looked at the little wiggling nub on the end of Andy's arm and he laughed out loud. Andy laughed too, and when Tony wiggled his pinky finger back at Andy, they both laughed even harder.

"I think they like each other," said Andy, and he started talking in a little high-pitched voice as if the nub on the end of his arm was talking to Tony's baby finger.

Tony picked right up on it, and the two of them talked back and forth in pretend voices as if they were putting on a puppet show.

"Hey," said Andy, "You're good at this. Are you here for acting too? I'm on a drama scholarship."

"No," said Tony. "I'm here on an art scholarship. I'm going to do pottery all week. I can't act for anything. I have such a rotten memory, I'd make a fool of myself."

"You sure could act when you were talking through your little finger!" said Andy.

"Aw, I was just kidding around. That wasn't acting."

"Sure it was. It's called *improvisation*. You make stuff up as you go along. And you're good at it. I bet you could act if you wanted to." Andy got quiet and looked down at his left arm. "Not like me and pottery," he said. "I've always thought making stuff with clay would be so cool. But no matter how much I want to, I could never make a pot on a potter's wheel."

"Don't be so sure about that," said Tony. "I get this art magazine and I once read about a guy who lost an arm in an accident and he taught himself to use the potter's wheel with only one arm. If you want, I can try to show you how he did it."

"Okay," said Andy. "But only if you try out for this week's play!"

"Geez," said Tony. "I don't know if I can memorize lines in one week."

"I'll go over your lines with you and you'll go over the clay with me and we'll both do something we never dreamed of doing."

"And always dreaded," Tony mumbled. "Andy, I'm afraid of getting up in front of people. Do you really think I can do it?"

"Do you really think I can learn to use the potter's wheel?"

"OK, I get it," said Tony. "If you're willing to try, so am I."

The two new friends worked together all that week. First Tony had to teach himself how to throw a pot one-handed—and it wasn't easy! Clay flew off the wheel and hit the wall—one hunk even hit Andy in the stomach. By the end of the first session, the two of them looked like mud pies with legs—and great big smiles. Tony did manage to get one little piece of clay to stay on the wheel and actually look like a pot. He found that if he put his left hand in his back pocket, it helped the rest of his body to get the right pressure on the clay.

"I think I've got it," said Tony. "Next time, you'll try."

The next day, after they got the wheel going with the clay on it, Tony said, "Just put your hand on mine so you can feel what's happening."

"It's wiggling all over the place," giggled Andy. "How do you get it to settle down?"

"That's the hardest part," Tony answered, as he put pressure in just the right place to center the clay. When it was centered, Tony took the clay off the wheel and threw it back down again. "Now let's try it with your hand on the bottom," said Tony. Andy put his hand on the wet clay and with a little help from Tony's hand on top, they got the clay ball centered.

"I can't believe it," said Andy. "Will you look at this!"

"Well it's not a pot yet, but I bet it will be by tomorrow. You really caught on fast. Now what about my acting lesson? Tryouts are tonight."

It was almost as if each boy got two weeks for one that summer. Andy was learning to do something he had always dreamed of and never thought was possible, and Tony was learning to memorize lines and speak in front of people—something he had always been afraid to do. On the last day, Tony had managed to memorize the lines for his small part, but he was still practicing them as he guided Andy through the making of one more pot to take home to show his parents. The two boys were working so hard, they never heard Billy and Chuck come in through the door.

"Wow! Will you look at that!" exclaimed Chuck. "So that's how you do it!"

"Do what?" said Tony and Andy almost together.

"That pot!" said Chuck. "That's why I could never get it right. I've always been using two hands. Nobody ever told me I was only supposed to use one!"

Tony and Andy looked at each other and started laughing so hard they couldn't catch their breath.

"What's so funny?" asked Chuck. "What did I say?"

"Should we tell them?" asked Andy.

"It's your pot, Andy," said Tony. "You show them how it's done!"

—JUDITH C. CAMPBELL

An Almost Awful Holiday

Hey Mom," called Raychel as she burst through the door after school, "Can Sooze stay over tonight? She's really upset because this is the first holiday after her parents' divorce, and she has to go to her dad's with his new wife and her two boys, and even though she wants to see her dad, she doesn't want to be with them . . . and her dad is saying things like she should get to like them because those two boys are her brothers now and . . . ."

"Raychel," her mother interrupted, "take a breath!"

Raychel took a breath and sat down at the kitchen table. "I just feel so bad for Sooze," she said. "Sooze always hoped that her parents would get back together, but now her dad has a new wife and she has to be part of a whole new family—and she doesn't even like boys!"

"Divorce is really hard on everybody," said Raychel's mother, "especially in the beginning. It's hard on the grown-ups because they're sad that their plans to be married forever didn't work out. And it's hard on the kids, because they have absolutely no say in what their parents decide to do. And maybe what's hardest of all is that nothing is the same as it was before the divorce—for anyone."

"So what can we do?" pleaded Raychel.

"I think you're right to invite Sooze over," said her mom, "but Raychel, let her do the talking—and only if she wants to. The best thing we can do is listen. We can't change what's happening in Sooze's family, but we can be her friends."

"You and daddy aren't going to get a divorce are you?" asked Raychel in a worried voice. "You fight sometimes."

"No. Your dad and I do have arguments and sometimes we can get pretty loud, but any two people living together are going to disagree sometimes. Divorce happens when bad feelings run so deep that living together makes both grown-ups really unhappy. Daddy and I are happy living together. But Raychel, I can understand why you might worry, especially when you see what's happening to your best friend. Tell her to come on over, and we'll have pizza for supper."

"Thanks, Mom, you're the best."

"Hey Raych," said her mom smiling, "takes one to know one. I love you."

Sooze got to Raychel's house almost before Raychel had hung up the phone. But it was not the usual, bouncy, happy Sooze. This Sooze was quiet, and it looked as if she'd been crying. But for once, Raychel didn't say anything, she just went to the fridge, and got out the soda, while her mom went for the chips. It wasn't until after supper, when they were scraping cheese off the pizza box for the cat, that Sooze began to talk.

"So . . . um . . . well . . ." Sooze wanted to say something, but it was clear that she didn't know quite how to begin. "So, are you guys going to have your big family Christmas again this year? Is your dad going to cook a goose again?"

"Probably," sighed Raych, "I wish he would make a pizza or something."

"Not for Christmas dinner!" said Sooze, looking horrified.

"Why not? I'd even rather have peanut butter!"

"How about frog's legs?" said Sooze, joining the game.

"Or squid, or octopus," added Raychel. "Yuk!"

The two girls started to giggle, but Sooze's giggles soon turned into sobs and before Raychel could stop laughing, Sooze was crying her eyes out. "I'd eat dirt for Christmas dinner if I could just do it with both my parents and I'm Jewish—I don't even celebrate Christmas! We have Hanukkah—that means I'll have eight whole days with daddy's new wife and her two dumb kids. Oh Raychel, I don't want to go," Sooze sobbed.

Raychel's mother was standing in the doorway and she heard Sooze pouring out her sadness to Raychel. She came into the kitchen, and sat down between the two girls.

"Sooze, do you have to go to your dad's?" Raychel's mom asked softly.

Sooze nodded "yes." And then she whispered, "The judge said I have to. We have to take turns on the holidays."

"Okay," said Raychel's mom, taking a deep breath, "so going to your dad's is something you have no choice about. But maybe there are some other choices you can make."

"Like what?" wondered Raychel.

"Well, let's talk about your week with your dad, Sooze. What part do you think is going to be the hardest for you?"

Sooze was still crying as she said, "I'm supposed to call Dad's wife 'Mom' and I don't want to. I have my own mom. And I have to share a room with her two kids. Plus, my real mom will be all alone, and I won't get to see you guys like we always do."

"Can't you tell your dad how you feel?" asked Raychel.

"I don't know," said Sooze. "I'm afraid Dad will get mad, or I'll hurt his feelings if I tell him how I feel."

"Sooze," said Raychel's mom, "your dad has not stopped loving you just because he and your mom got divorced. I know your dad and he's a great guy. I know that he respects your feelings. But he's not a mind reader; you have to tell him how you feel. What your dad wants most of all is to spend happy time with you."

Sooze thought quietly for a minute. "I could tell him I'll bring my sleeping bag and sleep on the sofa in the living room. And I could ask him if it was okay if I called his new wife Claire, instead of Mom," Sooze said.

"And Sooze, we'll have your mom here with us," said Raychel's mom, "so she won't be all alone. You could call us in the afternoon, and we'll put you on the speaker phone so we can all talk to you."

"And tell you how great the yukky goose is," interrupted Raychel.

"That would be so great," said Sooze. "And, I wonder if I could go for just four days instead of all eight?" she said, "That wouldn't be so bad. I could go for another four days some other time."

"Why don't you ask your dad?" said Raychel's mom. "And when you do, tell him how you feel, and why you feel that way."

"I'll try," Sooze said, "and maybe I can make the potato latkes before I go so I know at least one thing will taste good at Hanukkah dinner! You know, maybe this isn't going to be the worst holiday ever. There are some things that I can do to make it better. But first, I have to call my dad—can I use the telephone?"

—JUDITH C. CAMPBELL

The Coat That Came for Christmas

More than anything in the world, Josie wanted a new winter coat this Christmas, one with lots of pockets and zippers like all the other kids wore. She knew better than to ask her mother for it because there just wasn't enough money for that sort of thing. But one afternoon, on the bus ride home from school, she did tell her friend Raychel Morgan.

When Josie and her family moved to town, Raychel's church had "adopted" Josie's family so they could help the Rodriguezes adjust to a new life in a new country. Raychel was asked to show Josie around school and they soon became fast friends. Josie was Hispanic and her real name was Josefina Rodriguez. When Josie's mother said her name, she said "Hosefina Rrodriheth," and she called Raychel, "Rrra-hel." Raych thought that her Spanish accent made ordinary American words sound mysterious and special. But Josie didn't think anything about her family was mysterious and special, she just felt different. Different because she spoke Spanish at home, and when she spoke English it was with a Spanish accent. And she felt different because her family had very little money. Any Christmas presents Josie got would come from a church or a social worker—and they would not be new. They would be nice things, but she would know they had belonged to someone else first.

"Hey, Rachel," Josie said, "What are you going to get for Christmas?"

"Oh, I never know," answered Raych, "my parents usually get me something that's good for me, and some fun stuff too. How about you?"

"I want a new jacket," said Josie, and she quickly turned her head toward the window so Raych couldn't see her face. "A brand-new jacket, so new the tags will still be on it." Raychel knew Josie's mother couldn't afford a new jacket.

"You know, Josie," Raych replied, "the jacket I'm wearing isn't very old and it's getting small for me. Maybe my mom would let me give this one to you."

Josie turned the saddest face toward Raychel that she had ever seen. "Raych, don't you see? That jacket will always be your jacket. Even if you give it to me, and I wear it, the kids at school will say 'There goes Josie wearing Raychel's old jacket.' I want a jacket that nobody has ever worn before . . . just once."

Raychel's mother and other people at church had been helping Josie's family with donations of clothes and food and babysitting. She had been thinking about what they could give Josie for Christmas and now she knew!

"Ma!" Raychel called out as she burst through the door, "I just found out what Josie wants for Christmas. She wants a new jacket."

"Well good," replied her mother, "I'm sure someone at church will have a nice jacket that one of their kids has outgrown. We'll find one that will fit Josie perfectly."

"No, Mom," said Raychel, "it has to be a new jacket." And Raychel told her mother about the conversation she and Josie had on the bus. "I've never seen anyone look so sad, Mom. Can't we get her a new jacket?"

"Oh, Raych," sighed her mom, "this is tricky. I'd love to say yes, but there are a couple of problems. First of all, we were thinking of buying *you* a new jacket this Christmas and we couldn't afford to buy two. But even if we could, we have to consider Josie's mother's feelings. She has a lot to be proud of—raising three kids all by herself, working full-time to provide for them, as well as going to school herself. It might make her feel bad if we gave Josie such a big gift. It might remind her of what she can't do right now for her family."

Raychel was quiet for a minute. Having something new was so important to Josie and Raychel really wanted to give her friend the thing that would make her most happy. But how? Then it hit her.

"Mom," Raychel began, "what if *I* give Josie the new jacket you were planning on buying me? I can wait another year for a new jacket. You could tell her mother it was my idea and my choice. Do you think that would be OK?"

Raychel's mother smiled, "I can't imagine anyone turning down such a generous gift."

"Can I help pick it out? Can we go shopping right now?" Raychel bubbled with excitement.

"Sure you can. Let's go!" her mom answered. As they climbed in the car, it was hard to tell who was happier about this plan—Raychel or her mom.

The store was packed with holiday shoppers, most of whom seemed to be buying new jackets! But before long Raychel and her mom found the perfect one. It was deep red, with patches of purple and blue on the pockets, and zippers everywhere—just like the ones all the kids were wearing at school. For one tiny minute Raych wished she was getting the new jacket, but the tingling feeling she got when she imagined Josie's surprise and joy having the new jacket was much stronger. This was a new feeling for Raychel and she liked it.

"Is this for you, or should I wrap it?" asked the salesclerk.

"It was supposed to be for me, but I'm giving it to my friend instead. She's never had a new jacket before. It's going to be a surprise for her," Raychel rattled on. "But I'd like to wrap it myself, please."

"Boy, that's the true spirit of Christmas," the sales clerk replied, as she double-checked the Morgan's phone number and address on the check Raychel's mother had given her. "It's contagious, you know? Merry Christmas," she said, smiling and handing the package to Raychel.

"What did she mean, 'it's contagious'?" asked Raychel on their way home.

"Well, contagious means "catching." In this case, I think the saleslady meant that when one person is really generous and really gives from the heart, then it makes other people want to do the same. It's like the Magic Penny song we sang in church last week."

116

It's just like a magic penny.

Hold it tight and you won't have any.

Lend it, spend it, and you'll have so many,

they'll roll all over the floor.

Raychel joined in with the chorus,

Cause love is something if you give it away,

you end up having more.

It seemed to take forever, but Christmas day finally arrived. Josie's mom had happily agreed to keep the gift a surprise and put it under the tree Christmas Eve after Josie was asleep. Christmas morning, as Raychel and her family opened their gifts, they all wondered silently: Had Josie opened the package yet? Did she like the jacket? Did it fit?

They didn't have to wait long for their answer. Halfway through breakfast the doorbell rang.

"I wonder who that is?" said Raychel's dad. Raychel answered the door. It was Josie, in her beautiful new jacket with a plate of bizcichitos, the delicious Spanish Christmas cookies Josie's mother made every year.

"Come in, come in," squealed Raych, "let me see it on you!"

"My mother told me what you did, Raychel," Josie said as she entered. "This is the nicest gift anyone has ever given me. I just love this jacket and I can't thank you enough." And she gave Raychel a big hug.

"I'm glad you like it," Raychel replied, "I had a lot of fun picking it out for you and thinking about you getting it and . . ."

"Wait, don't close the door," Josie interrupted, "there's a package out here on your doorstep. It's all wrapped up and it says 'to Miss Morgan.'"

Raychel's mother and father looked at each other. Each was silently saying to the other, "Did you?" "No. Did you?" "No." "Well then, who?" "And, what?"

Raychel took the box and started unwrapping it: first brown paper, then Christmas wrap, and then a box with tape holding it together and layers of tissue paper inside. Raych thought she'd never get to it, but finally the last bit of tissue came away, and there in the box was another new jacket! It was beautiful, with white faux fur around the collar, silver buttons, and silver fringe on one shoulder, and lots of pockets and zippers. Raychel was speechless.

Her parents were still saying things like, "I didn't, you didn't, well who on earth did?" when Raychel spotted a card in the pocket of the jacket. "What's this?" she wondered and she pulled out a plain, white envelope with her name on it. The card was a simple, folded one, with a single gold star on the front. She opened it up and slowly read, "To Miss Morgan, Thanks for helping me catch the spirit. Merry Christmas."

—JUDITH C. CAMPBELL

The Christmas Without Gram

I t was not going to be a good Christmas this year. Raych knew that and so did Beezer. Raych's grandmother had died right after Thanksgiving. This would be the first Christmas without her. Beezer was Gram's dog, and he didn't understand. He kept going to the door every time he heard a car in the driveway, and then slinking back to the place beside the chair that Gram always sat in. Raych sat in that chair now, remembering Gram. Gram was her special friend. She listened when the other grown-ups were too busy. The grown-ups did not understand. They were almost acting as if nothing had happened . . . almost.

Raychel felt so sad. Beezer was so sad he wasn't even stealing things any more. Beezer was a thief! He loved to "find" things and bring them home. Gram was forever trying to find the children in the neighborhood who belonged to the toys and hats and mittens that Beezer dragged home.

Christmas was getting closer. Raych felt very mixed up. At the same time she felt sad about Gram, she also felt some happy thoughts about Christmas. Then she wondered if this was a bad thing. How could she have two feelings at the same time? She missed Gram and she still liked Christmas. She really wished Gram were here to talk about it. When something was troubling her, Gram would always say "Let's talk about it," and somehow that made it better. Raych tried talking to her cousin Tony, but it wasn't the same.

Then, as if things weren't bad enough, two days before Christmas, Beezer went out and didn't come back. Raychel's mom and dad called all around the neighborhood. Nothing worked. Beezer was missing. Raych felt even sadder than when they told her that Gram had died. Beezer was all she had left of Gram and now it seemed that even he was gone. That night, Raych got ready for bed wishing she could start this whole year over again and have it come out nice, the way it did in the storybooks and on TV.

Suddenly, she heard something scratching at the door. She raced downstairs and opened the door. There was Beezer, and he had something in his mouth. Beezer, the thief, had brought her a "gift." He walked in and put the "gift" on the floor at Raych's feet. It moved ever so slightly, and then it meowed! Beezer had brought home the wettest, coldest, hungriest little cat Raych had ever seen. She picked it up and ran in to show her parents. They were happy about Beezer, but they weren't sure about a wet sick cat that might not live. No one knew quite what to do with the cat. They fed it milk and put it in a box near the stove.

The next morning, the kitten and the dog were not to be found. They had to be in the house somewhere, and Raych was the first to find them over in the corner near the heater in the room where Gram used to stay. The cat was much more lively than it had been the night before. Raych called out the news of her discovery to her parents, and the whole family stood and watched as a large and gentle dog softly washed life and love back into a still skinny, but loudly purring cat.

"I think we've just seen a miracle," whispered Raychel's dad. His voice had that funny sound it always had when he was having very strong feelings about something.

But there was still lots to do if they were going to be ready for the rest of the family when they arrived for Christmas Eve dinner. "The one without Gram," thought Raych, "but, maybe it won't be so bad after all. My cousin Tony will be here and Beezer is finally beginning to act like himself again."

After dinner, the family stories began. So many of them started with, "Gram would have . . ." or, "Do you remember when she . . ." that Raych couldn't listen to any more. She quietly crept upstairs to the room where Gram used to stay. She shut the door and let her tears say all that was in her heart.

She didn't hear the door push open behind her, but she did feel the nudge of a large furry head against her leg. She reached down without really looking and rubbed old Beezer behind his ear. He nudged her again and she looked down to see that he had brought the little cat to her. Raychel knelt down on the floor beside Beezer and the cat, laughing and crying and trying to hug Beezer all at the same time. Beezer seemed to understand, and so did she, that Gram would have loved this moment.

Raychel was feeling so sad, and Beezer was trying to help. And if Beezer was trying so hard to help her, maybe she should start to help herself as well.

The three of them went downstairs to the rest of the family, and told the story of Beezer's "gift." "Now this seems normal," said Tony, "a Beezer story complete with the evidence. So, what are you going to call it?"

"First of all," said Raych, "the cat is a boy, and the vet said that he is missing two toes."

"Missing toes," said Tony, "at Christmastime? How about calling him Mistletoe?" Everyone, including Raychel, groaned. Raych decided to leave the final vote to Beezer. She put the kitten on the floor at Beezer's feet, and asked him if the name "Mistletoe" was going to be good enough for their cat. Beezer lowered his lumpy head and licked the cat and then, ever so gently, he lifted Mistletoe in his great, soft mouth and gave him to Raych. Everybody smiled and wiped away tears at the same time. "Mistletoe it is then," said Raychel's dad, "and will you all look outside?"

The icy rain that had been falling for two days had turned to snow. It was a very, very special Christmas this year. And the more Raychel thought about it, the more she realized things were just the way Gram would have wanted them!

—JUDITH C. CAMPBELL

About the Contributors

CHARLENE BROTMAN is the author of the UUA curriculum *Focus on Noah* and the co-author, with Ann Fields and Barbara Marshman, of *Why Do Bad Things Happen?*, *How Can I Know What to Believe?*, *Holidays and Holy Days*, and *The UU Kids Book*. Brotman began writing curricula because she wanted to give her young daughter an understanding of the Bible from a Unitarian Universalist perspective.

JUDITH C. CAMPBELL is the minister of the UU Society of Martha's Vineyard, Massachusetts. Previously she taught art for twenty-seven years at Lesley University in Cambridge, Massachusetts. Campbell is the author of two books on watercolor painting; *Let's Talk about It*, a collection of children's stories; and *The Stuff of Life*, a collection of poems, prayers, and reflections on everyday life. In addition to her passion for writing, she continues to make and exhibit contemporary wall quilts and watercolor paintings.

ANN FIELDS led religious education programs at Unitarian Universalist congregations in Medfield, Concord, Arlington, and Belmont, Massachusetts. She was a counselor and mentor to many who now serve as professional leaders in Unitarian Universalist communities. She taught religious education courses at Harvard Divinity School and served for four years on the UUA staff as the children's programs director. Fields collaborated with Barbara Marshman and Charlene Brotman to write and edit many curricula still widely used in Unitarian Universalist congregations, including *Holidays and Holy Days*.

SOPHIA LYON FAHS was a progressive educator and author of many UU religious education curricula and books for children, most notably *From Long Ago and Many Lands* and *The Church Across the Street*. The Martin and Judy stories, which realized Fahs's dream of a religious education that begins with children's first-hand experiences, were a model for *uu&me!* From 1937 to 1961, Fahs was editor of curriculum materials for religious education for the American Unitarian Association.

NOREEN KIMBALL has been in magazine and newsletter publishing for thirty years. Early in her career she spent three years as assistant managing editor of *UUWorld* and has been a contributing writer for *uu&me!* since 1998.

BARBARA MARSHMAN served Unitarian Universalism as a minister of religious education for more than fifty years, in congregations in Medford, Winchester, and Lexington, Massachusetts. She collaborated with Ann Fields and Charlene Brotman to write and edit many curricula still widely used in Unitarian Universalist congregations, including *Holidays and Holy Days*.

HEATHER B. MCDONALD is a member of the Don Heights Unitarian Congregation in Toronto, Canada, where she served as church school director for seventeen years. She has also directed or taught religious education in congregations in Winnepeg, Canada, and Hackensack, New Jersey, and served on the St. Lawrence District Religious Education Committee. McDonald's favorite exercise, in her more limber days, was ballet, and she is proud to have passed levels three and four in adult examinations in Russian-style ballet schools.

BARB PITMAN is a member of First Universalist Unitarian Church in Denver, Colorado, where she has served as board secretary, chaired a committee studying new forms of governance for the church, and started a children's choir. Pitman is the mother of three grown children, and she enjoys collecting anything "cape cod-ish," including lighthouses, shells, and wooden fish.

KENNETH SAWYER grew up in New Jersey. Since 1974 he has been the minister of First Parish in Wayland, Massachusetts. In addition to many years of service to Unitarian Universalist-related committees and organizations, Sawyer has co-taught a course on preaching at Harvard Divinity School and co-authored the textbook *Thematic Preaching*. He and his wife have grown twin daughters and two grandchildren, who also live in Wayland.

DOROTHY SPOERL's held dual ministerial fellowship with the Universalist Church of America and the American Unitarian Association and served many churches in both organizations as either minister or director of religious education. Spoerl's career included five years as editor of the Beacon Series, followed by four years as curriculum editor at the UUA. In 1987 Spoerl received the UUA Distinguished Service Award and in 1994 she received the Angus MacLean Award in Religious Education.

VALERIE WHITE is the vice president of the Unitarian Church of Sharon, Massachusetts. She has served on the board of the Church of the Larger Fellowship, as treasurer of Unitarian Universalists for Jewish Awareness, and in the pulpit of a congregation in Vermont during a ministerial search. White sang in a church choir when she lived in Vermont, and she loves to teach children to ride horseback.

BETSY HILL WILLIAMS has been writing for children and families for the past ten years as director of religious education at the Church of the Larger Fellowship of the Unitarian Universalist Association. Her published work includes *Religious Education at Home, Cycle of Seasons, Women of Courage*, and *Waldo, Free and True*. She enjoys the freelance writer's life (write a little, ski a little; write a little, garden a little) in Harvard with her husband, their two college-age children, and an assortment of animals, including chickens and pigs.